Diann,
hope you enjoy my stories and have fun cooking with my favorite recipes!

Lani

NOSTALGIC FEAST

tales and recipes from a lifetime
pursuit of pleasing people's palates

by Laurel Lather

st. john's press

Published by st. john's press
www.stjohnspress.com

All rights reserved. No part of this book may be reproduced in any form by any electronic or mechanical means (including photocopying, recording, or information storage and retrieval) without permission in writing from the publisher.

For more information and bulk sales, please email info@stjohnspress.com.

©2021 by Laurel Lather

Library of Congress Cataloging-in-Publication Data
Laurel Lather
Nostalgic Feast: ...tales and Recipes from a Lifetime Pursuit of Pleasing People's Palate
Library of Congress Control Number: 2021917741

ISBN 978-1-955027-04-5 (hardback)
ISBN 978-1-955027-05-2 (e-book)

Editor-in-Chief: Torund Bryhn
Editor: Richard Willett
Creative Design Director: Yamilca Rodriguez
Designer: Camila Ramirez
Photography (Book Cover): Brittany Elizabeth Images
Printed and bound in the United States of America.

st. john's press

stjohnspress.com

info@stjohnspress.com

dedication

I dedicate this book to my dearly departed grandparents, Dick and Helen, whose inspiring passion encouraged me to follow a path that opened the door to adventures I could never have imaged…and to my husband, Doug, whose never ending support keeps me on this journey.

praise

"A TREASURE – Delightful and heartwarming memories shared by an exceptional Chef. Her words allow our minds to go back to childhood experiences in our own Mother's kitchens, once again remembering the smells and sounds of her cooking. This book is a must-have…if not for the memories, for the fabulous recipes!"

-Teri Schmidt

Executive Director

Experience Sioux Falls

"I love, love LOVE this book! Laurel's lifelong passion, creativity and entrepreneurial spirit make for a most entertaining read. Weaving her recipes into her journey brings each flavorful creation to life and makes me want to try every single one! What an amazing life story of a most accomplished woman."

-Mary Yungeberg

Author

The Rowan Milani Chronicles

"Every memorable meal has a great story to go with it, and Laurel Lather cooks up both with this look at her culinary journey. We're lucky it wound through Sioux Falls, where she built a well-deserved reputation as a sought-after chef whose restaurants filled with regulars, that I know will enjoy this latest "Feast!""

-Jodi Schwan

Publisher

SiouxFalls.Business

acknowledgements

First and foremost, I would like to express all my gratitude to Terry & Lynette Kelley, James Jacobson, Albert Brooks, Tom & Becky Stritecky, Brad & Lori Olson for believing in my visions and talent. I was fortunate to have you as partners, learning something unique from each of you. Without you these stories would not exist.

To all my friends, family, employees, and customers who supported my dream, I will always treasure our shared experiences. I thank you for your committed loyalty.

The devotion shown from my wine and food reps throughout the years is something I never took for granted. You were all a joy to work with. A few of you deserve special appreciation for going above and beyond. Jim Eckert, for twenty years you were by my side, accepting all the challenges to locate hard to find ingredients for me. John Thuringer and Shauna Wallace, all the extra hours spent doing taste research and the help with special events, was instrumental in my education and success. Jethe Lowman Abdouch, your fortitude was motivating, your sense of humor could quell all my stresses. I will always value all of you for your talents and friendship.

And to fate, who brought Torund Bryhn into my life, I hope that you continue to dangle my destiny in front of me at just the right time. This book would never have come to be without her expertise and guidance.

Delving into the unknown can easily be overwhelming but working with Torund and her team was an educational experience so well-orchestrated that I felt comfortable in this new endeavor. Richard Willett was a precise editor, teaching me to be more detailed in expressing my thoughts. Zachary Houghton, who I would call the tech-guy, was patient with my lack of understanding web-site building details. I knew that taking all my photographs, stories and recipes would be a huge challenge to any designer, but Camila Ramirez was astounding at making my vision a reality. Yamilca Rodriguez's organization between all these creative professionals was an amazing site to watch unfold.

I thank you all for believing in this project.

table of contents

Preface .... p. 8

Chapter 1: the beginning .... p. 11

Chapter 2: spreading my wings .... p. 25

Chapter 3: expanding my horizons .... p. 35

Chapter 4: time to step into management .... p. 45

Chapter 5: getting back to entrepreneurism .... p. 57

Chapter 6: time to put the chef's coat back on .... p. 69

Chapter 7: taking on a bigger project .... p. 85

Chapter 8: back on my feet .... p. 99

Chapter 9: my crowning glory .... p. 121

Chapter 10: dealing with a pandemic .... p. 217

Epilogue .... p. 231

Laurel Lather's Bio .... p. 234

Praise .... p. 235

Recipe Index .... p. 238

preface

"A recipe is a story that ends with a good meal." -Pat Conroy

I was fortunate to have been brought up in a freestyle environment. There wasn't a box full of toys; I had to discover ways to entertain myself. You'd find me in the gardens, the kitchen cupboards, or in my rocking chair reading books. Independence and creativity were nurtured.

While we sat at the dinner table, the stories of the day were told. When we came in off the lake after fishing, the most fun was sharing the tales of the one that got away. The teachers commented on my report cards that I was a very curious girl who loved to participate during show-and-tell time. This thread was woven throughout my life.

It's always been about the story . . .

Many of the recipes you will find in this book are comfort foods, dishes that trigger an emotional response. Bite after bite, memories of when you enjoyed this taste intensify. The stories I have shared are nostalgic for me. You can eat the same dish and an entirely different sentimental memory will come to mind.

This is one of the reasons that my passion for food went beyond my own kitchen to wanting to share my enthusiasm with others. I don't believe in eating for the sole purpose of sustenance. It is something that should be enjoyed as a social event. This doesn't mean that you must go out to diners and restaurants all the time. I want to inspire you to prepare chef-quality dishes in your own home.

For those of you that are beginning cooks, don't let the recipe overwhelm you. If you try to overthink each step, frustration will take over. Follow your heart, not your brain. A recipe is a guideline, not set in stone. If you don't like an ingredient, leave it out or replace it with something else. Let your personal taste lead the way.

For those of you who have eaten at my restaurants and requested a lot of the recipes, I am thrilled that you can now take your favorites and make them your own. I may not be bringing good food to you through brick and mortar any longer, but hopefully this culinary narrative keeps my pursuit of pleasing people's palates alive.

Laurel Lather

Chapter One

the beginning

culinary inspiration from my grandparents as a child...

This is when it all started . . . sitting in a highchair, next to the mangle that was adorned with a lace doily and Grandpa's radio. Gramma Helen bustling about in the warm kitchen, kneading dough, chopping vegetables, and boiling bones. The sound of spoons jingling in her pinafore pocket was barely heard over the static-interrupted music. I was entertained by this daily ritual, cooing when a tasting tidbit would be offered on my tray.

I finally graduated to the Cosco step stool, where I could be by her side. I watched as she dropped ingredient after ingredient into a pot, not all at once, but with some mysterious timing that only she knew. Gramma put everything under my nose, sometimes just one ingredient, then combining two. "See how they smell so good together," she would say. Unknowingly, my culinary education had begun.

gardening roots and preserving vegetables...

The passion for food continued to grow throughout my childhood. Grandpa Dick took me into his greenhouse and taught me all about gardening. He had large hands, so watching him place the tiny seeds into the dirt and helping the plants with pollination amazed me.

Harvest time was my favorite. Gramma would hold out the skirt of her apron, laughing as I filled it with vegetables, so full she could barely walk. After a thorough spraying with the hose, we would sort them in wicker baskets and get ready for canning.

Tomatoes, corn, and beets were crammed into jars, boiled in large pots, then set out to cool. The lids popping as they sealed were almost like notes to a song. The aroma of vinegar burned my nostrils as pots of brine for dilly beans and pickled beets simmered.

Grandpa always manned the large wooden kraut cutter, masterfully slicing head after head of cabbage. After filling the tin wash tub, he would generously salt the cabbage, pounding with his fists until he started expelling moisture. From there it took the trip down to the storm cellar to be stuffed into the Red Wing crocks for fermenting.

sauerkraut

2 heads green cabbage, thinly sliced
¼ cup kosher salt
2 tablespoons caraway seeds
6 ounces lager beer

Put the cabbage in a big bowl and sprinkle it with salt, massaging and pounding the cabbage with your hands until it starts to get limp. Toss in caraway seeds.

Put in a plastic bucket, large glass container or crock. Pour in the beer, then enough water to cover all the cabbage. Use a plate and clean rocks to weigh it down. Cover with a cloth.

Store out of direct sunlight and under 65 degrees for about a week. It will bubble and foam, that is normal, so do not fill containers all the way to the top.

Makes 2 – 3 quarts

Then it was pickle time, my favorite! We layered dill and the larger pickling cucumbers in crocks, then filled jars with the smaller-sized cukes, for kosher, sweet gherkins, and bread and butter pickles.

bread and butter pickles

12 english cucumbers, cut into ¼-inch slices
2 yellow onions, thinly sliced
4 tablespoons pickling salt
2 cups rice wine vinegar
2 quarts apple cider vinegar
1 quart water
2 cups sugar
¼ cup pickling spice
10 whole cloves
3 tablespoons yellow mustard seed
1 tablespoon red pepper flakes
1 tablespoon celery seed
1 tablespoon coriander seed
¼ teaspoon turmeric

Place the cucumber slices and onion in a bowl and toss with the pickling salt. Let sit while making the brine. To make the brine, combine the remaining ingredients in a large stockpot, and bring to a hard boil. Pour over the cucumbers and toss well. Put it in the refrigerator. The pickles will be ready in 24 hours.

Makes 3 – 4 quarts

red wine pickles

12 english cucumbers, cut into ¼-inch slices
8 green onions, thinly sliced
4 tablespoons himalayan pink sea salt
4 cups red wine vinegar
1 cup water
1 750-milliliter bottle petite verdot wine
4 cups sugar
2 tablespoons minced garlic
2 tablespoons crushed pink peppercorns
2 tablespoons pickling spice

Place the cucumber slices and onion in a bowl and toss with the salt. Let sit while making the brine. To make the brine, combine the remaining ingredients in a large stockpot and bring to a hard boil. Pour over the cucumbers and toss well. Put it in the refrigerator. The red color will set in after 24 hours.

Makes 3 – 4 quarts

sunday traditions...

I had so much fun being Gramma's little helper, but I was waiting for the time that I would get the chance to make something myself. That morning finally arrived, and it was not with her, but for her!

Sunday was traditionally church and chore day. We would drive to the town of Hancock, Wisconsin, so Gramma could go to church while Grandpa and I did errands. We would do the weekly drop-off at the dump, pick up supplies, then stop in at the local tavern. By the time I managed to climb up onto the old worn leather stool, the barkeep would have our bottles of Point beer and cream soda waiting. We'd share a package of blind robins and play bar dice. But from the beginning this Sunday was going to be different. Grandpa had a trick up his sleeve.

Blind Robins

Blind robins are tiny, individual smoked and salted herring, very much like fish jerky, wild-caught off Canada's coast, packaged with a picture of a blue blindfolded bird. Along with being a bar snack meant to increase consumption, they can also be used for a touch of umami in creamy soups or egg dishes.

Before the sun even peeked over the horizon, I was quietly awakened to share a secret plan to surprise Gramma with breakfast in bed. On the menu were rhubarb scones with strawberry jam and bacon. A quick trip to the garden yielded a basket full of rhubarb and strawberries. The well-used, tattered recipe card was clipped to the cupboard to avoid the impending mess.

We carefully measured all the dry ingredients into a big stoneware bowl. I mixed it by tossing it about as if it were snow. The butter was cut in small pieces and sat in a bowl of ice water while Grandpa met the milkman coming up the driveway. As I was smashing the butter into the flour mix, he slowly started adding the fresh cream and eggs. "Don't play too much with the dough," he warned, "or they'll be too chewy!" With the final addition of the rhubarb, we had a sticky dough that hung heavily from my fingers.

Deciding not to roll out the dough, we instead made odd shapes like rocks and laid them on the sheet for baking. After a light brushing of egg yolk beaten with a splash of rosewater and a sprinkle of sugar, they were ready for the oven. As they baked, we fried bacon strips, carefully pouring the remaining fat into a coffee can, and cooked the strawberries down with honey for a quick jam.

When the tray was all arranged with tea and flowers, Grandpa carried it while I opened the door to their bedroom and jumped on the bed. "Wake up, wake up," I gleefully yelled. The three of us sat under the covers together, dropping crumbs all over the blankets. She gave me big hugs and kisses, saying how proud she was of me. This was my first solo kitchen flight not under her wings.

rhubarb scones

2¾ cups flour
½ cup sugar
1 tablespoon baking powder
1 teaspoon baking soda
½ teaspoon ginger
½ teaspoon salt
½ cup butter, cut into pieces
1 egg
¾ cup heavy cream
1½ cups diced rhubarb
1 egg yolk
¼ teaspoon rosewater
2 tablespoons sugar

Mix the flour, sugar, baking powder, baking soda, ginger, and salt in a large bowl. Add the butter pieces using your hands, mash it together until the mixture resembles coarse meal. Slowly add the egg and cream. Fold in the rhubarb.

Drop little handfuls of the dough onto a baking sheet lined with parchment paper. Beat the egg yolk with rosewater, lightly brush on the scone tops, and sprinkle with sugar. Bake in a 400-degree oven until a light golden brown, about 20 minutes.

Makes 12 – 16 scones

fresh strawberry jam

2 pounds fresh strawberries, sliced
1½ cups honey
zest and juice from 2 lemons

In a sauce pot, combine all the ingredients. While stirring, slowly bring the mixture to a boil. Cook for 25–30 minutes, stirring often so it doesn't burn. Skim off any foam that forms as it cools.

Makes 2 pints

chicken dinner...

Sunday dinner was always my favorite meal of the week. During football season, we put out a smorgasbord fit for a Packer kingdom, but that is another story, to be told later. During the off-season, our eating habits switched back to a traditional sit-down dinner.

Most of our meals were enjoyed in the living room in front of the old black-and-white Zenith. Grandpa would adjust the rabbit ears as I snapped the floral tops of the TV trays onto their legs. But Sunday was different. Dinner was an all-day production where each of us had a role. The dining table had to be stripped of its brightly colored cloth. The hand-embroidered linens were taken from the cedar chest, sprayed with rose-infused water, and then run through the mangle. The warm and fragrant cloth was adorned with Gramma's collection of blue Viking glassware and Currier and Ives dishes.

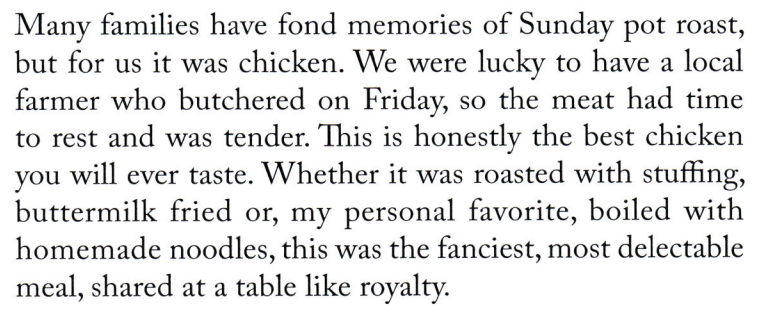

Many families have fond memories of Sunday pot roast, but for us it was chicken. We were lucky to have a local farmer who butchered on Friday, so the meat had time to rest and was tender. This is honestly the best chicken you will ever taste. Whether it was roasted with stuffing, buttermilk fried or, my personal favorite, boiled with homemade noodles, this was the fanciest, most delectable meal, shared at a table like royalty.

I remember my Gramma asking Grandpa to say grace. Instead he would toast, "I wonder what the poor folks are doing today." This was his way of expressing how blessed we were to sit at this table and share such wonderful food.

gramma helen's chicken and homemade noodles

2 yellow onions
1 head celery
1 whole chicken (remove giblets)
4 tablespoons celery salt
3 tablespoon thyme
18 bay leaves
3 tablespoons cracked black pepper
2 tablespoons garlic powder
2 tablespoons rubbed sage
1 cup plus 2 tablespoons flour
1 teaspoon salt
1 large egg
1 tablespoon milk
¾ stick butter

Prep vegetables and chicken: Take the skin off the onions and discard, remove and save the outer layer, and chop the remaining onion. Cut off the butt end of the celery and discard, trim and save the ends, and chop the remaining celery including the leaves.

Put the chicken, herbs and spices and saved onion/celery scraps in a stockpot, cover with water, bring to boil, then cover and let simmer until the meat falls off the bones, 1–2 hrs. Do not let your broth reduce by less than half; add water if necessary.

Make your noodles: While the chicken is cooking, mix the flour and salt, add the egg and milk, and mix with your hands to form into soft dough. On a floured surface knead the dough until silky, roll out to ⅛-inch-thick, cut in strips, cover with a light dusting of flour, and let rest.

Debone the chicken: When the meat falls off the bones and the broth has reduced by half, take off heat and let cool down enough to handle. Put a colander over a large bowl, pour all the ingredients from the stockpot into the colander, then pour the broth back into the stockpot. Pull the meat from the scraps and bones, leaving it in as large pieces as possible, and add it to the stock.

Sauté vegetables: Melt the butter in a sauté pan, add your chopped celery and onion along with an additional sprinkling of thyme and sage, cook until translucent, then add to the stock.

Add noodles: Bring your stockpot back to a boil, then add your noodles one at a time so they don't stick together. Sprinkle another 2 tablespoons of flour on top, stirring in right away so it doesn't clump.

Simmer: Once the noodles are cooked through, reduce heat to low and allow to simmer and thicken. Taste, and add any additional seasoning to your preference.

Serves 8

This recipe is one of my most cherished. Every time I make it there is a calmness that overcomes me, a feeling of family love. It was a special day when I finally got to teach my daughter, Jessica, how to make it.

great-gramma's influence...

A lot of our nostalgic experiences from when we were children are held warmly within our taste buds. They can be sparked by something as simple as the taste of the first candy you had, to the smell of your mom's chicken soup. These memories are usually the most intense, encompassing all your senses. A bite of apple pie can take you back to a moment; you can vividly see the person you shared it with, the place you were at, the aromas and sounds of that time.

Eating a certain meal can send you straight down memory lane. When I am missing the embrace of my Great-Gramma, there is one soup that I can make and suddenly I am in her home. An immigrant from Norway, she arrived with her soon-to-be husband in the port of Milwaukee. There they began their American experience together, staying in the same cozy home for their entire life.

Unfortunately, we couldn't make the long trip to visit often, so when we did, it was always a special treat. My Great-Gramma would be waiting for us on the front porch as the old pickup pulled up next to the curb. Her hugs were strong, holding you deep in her bosom where you could smell baking yeast and mustard that had been wiped into her apron. Immediately as you entered through the front door, you were hit with aromas of baking rye bread and corned beef. I would run to the kitchen right away.

When she lifted the lid from the soup pot, a salty, dill-laden steam escaped. Inside, yellow pearls bobbed in the boiling broth. This was whole yellow pea soup in the making, the only dish she ever made for us, and I wouldn't have wanted it any other way.

whole yellow pea soup

1½ pounds whole yellow peas, not split peas
1 tablespoon salt
6 carrots, small diced
8 stalks celery with leaves, chopped
1 yellow onion, diced
4 cup pork broth
¼ cup whole grain mustard
2 pounds cooked corned beef brisket
2 tablespoon bacon fat
1 (12-ounce) can lager
2 tablespoons minced garlic
1 tablespoon dill seed
4 bay leaves
½ tablespoon white pepper
2 tablespoons dill weed

Soak the whole yellow peas in water for at least 8 hours. I stress the importance of using whole peas, not split. The texture is more appealing, not a thick porridge, but a broth soup with bite, and they have a nuttier taste. Once they have soaked, rinse and put them in a stockpot. Cover with double the amount of water and sprinkle with salt. Slowly cook until al dente, adding extra water if needed so the peas are always covered. Remove half of the peas for later use.

Add the carrots, celery, onions, pork broth and mustard to the pot and continue to cook until the peas are popping out of their skins and beginning to thicken.

Stir in the remaining yellow peas and the corned beef, bacon fat, beer, and spices. Allow to simmer for another hour, adding additional water or stock if needed and salt and pepper to taste.

Serves 8

Chapter Two

spreading my wings

laurel's country herbs...

My Grandparents' marriage was a perfect blend of flora, fauna, and flavor. This combination, along with their entrepreneurial spirit, is what formed the soul of my life ambitions. So, at the age of 22, I decided to start my first business. Beginning with a plastic dome greenhouse and a half-acre plot of land just outside of Chippewa Falls, Wisconsin, Laurel's Country Herbs was born. With close to forty different varieties of herbs, the fragrance in the air drew customers off the country road. They could buy potted plants, pick their own fresh herbs, or purchase packets of dried seasonings and infused vinegars.

My customers' curiosity brought out the teacher in me. I thrived on that enthusiasm, teaching mothers in the Head Start program, who had to survive on subsidized foods, how to prepare their family meals using herbs and spices to bring out the best of the ingredients given to them. I spoke at Sacred Heart Hospital in Eau Claire to help cardiac patients lower the sodium in their diets.

Here are a few of the favorite herb blends from that time. They are best when fresh herbs are used, but dried herbs and spices ground together work just as well. I am a fan of using a mortar and pestle, but a coffee grinder lightly pulsed will speed up the process.

Handwritten Recipes

Whatever artistic skills I had were used to hand write and draw pages of recipes with basic information about the herbs and spices. While looking through boxes of memorabilia, I came across these old and yellowed pages. After forty years, I believe it is time to bring these relics back to life . . . my next project!

salt substitute

4 teaspoons sesame seed
3 teaspoons celery seed
2 teaspoons black peppercorns
1 teaspoon fennel seed
1 tablespoon parsley flakes
1 teaspoon onion flakes
⅛ teaspoon garlic granules

italian seasoning

3 tablespoons basil
2 tablespoons marjoram
3 tablespoons oregano
2 tablespoons rosemary
2 tablespoons thyme
1 tablespoon fennel seed
1 tablespoon red pepper flakes

zaatar for vegetables

1 tablespoon crushed thyme
1 tablespoon oregano
2 tablespoons sumac
1 tablespoon cumin seed
2 tablespoons coriander seed
1 tablespoon sesame seed
1 teaspoon red pepper flakes

herb de provence

2 tablespoons fennel seeds
2 tablespoons rosemary
4 tablespoons thyme
3 tablespoons summer savory
2 tablespoons tarragon
1 teaspoon mint
1 teaspoon chervil
3 tablespoons dried lavender

the general store...

I continued to speak for various women's organizations and was featured in the local newspaper often. The business's popularity was outgrowing my home location. When a downtown Chippewa Falls storefront became available, I jumped at the chance to expand my offerings. Working with area farmers, The General Store's concept of "back to basics" came to life.

In an old country setting, rows of Ball jars filled with freshly dried herbs lined the shelves. Bulk barrels with a huge variety of beans and rice were stacked against the brick walls.

Crates of locally grown produce and eggs were delivered daily. When you walked through the doors, you knew that all your cooking necessities would be met.

Not only did we share recipes, but we became a gathering spot for all area culinary specialists. In the back room, we sipped on cups of tea while sharing our skills. We inspired each other and allowed this dynamic to spill out into the services we offered our customers.

During this time, my use of cooking skills began to be more adventurous. A day spent out in the woods and fields with a forager opened my eyes to a new world of flavor beyond the typical herbs. One of my favorite new ingredients was something I had only previously put in vases—flowers!

Nasturtiums, pansies, roses, lavender, marigolds, violets, and lilacs are just a few of the popular flowers that have wonderful flavors and are underused as plate garnishes or cake décor. Many herb and vegetable blossoms have zesty flavors also. Be adventurous, but research first to avoid plucking poisonous buds or picking in an area that has been sprayed with pesticides.

Here is a list of some of the most popular edible flowers and their flavor:

- Bachelors Buttons—mild grassy flavors
- Bee Balm—not much flavor, used more for color
- Begonia flowers and leaves—citrusy with a hint of sour
- Borage flowers and leaves—cucumber flavor
- Calendula—not much flavor, used more for color
- Carnations—sweet to spicy flavor
- Chive blossoms and leaves—mild onion flavor
- Clover blossoms—sweet pea flavor
- Daisies—bitter flavor
- Dandelion greens and blossoms—bitter flavor
- Daylilies—sweet floral taste
- Fruit blossoms (apple, pear, plum, strawberry) – sweet floral taste
- Hibiscus—cranberry flavor
- Hollyhock petals and leaves—light vegetable flavor
- Honeysuckle blossoms, not the berries—sweet floral flavor
- Hosta flowers—sweet floral taste
- Lilac—sweet floral taste
- Nasturtium leaves and flowers—spicy
- Phlox—five-petaled blossoms are spicy
- Roses—taste just like they smell
- Scented geraniums—taste just like they smell
- Sunflower petals—mild taste, better for color
- Tulips—flavor varies from sweet to spicy, the red are the best
- Violets—sweet floral flavor

flower fritters

flowers (dandelions, daylilies, lilacs, tulips, squash, and pumpkin flowers are my favorites)
2 eggs
1 cup icy cold milk
1 cup flour
1 teaspoon sugar
½ teaspoon baking powder
oil for frying
salt and pepper

Clean the flowers in cold water and blot dry with a paper towel, making sure they are completely dry before frying.

Whisk the eggs and milk together, add the flour, sugar, and baking powder and mix until the batter is well blended.

> Hint: Remove the stamens and pistils from flowers before eating. Pollen can cause allergic reactions when eaten by some people, and it may overwhelm the otherwise delicate flavor of the petals.

Dip the flowers one at a time in the batter to lightly coat, letting the excess drip off.

Fry in the oil at 375 degrees until crisp and golden brown.

Drain on paper towels, and season with salt and pepper while they are still hot.

Delicious served with honey or herbed sour cream dip.

Makes 18 – 24 fritters

summer floral herb salad

4 ounces mixed greens
1 ounce mustard greens
1 ounce spinach
¼ cup arugula micro-greens
¼ cup chopped fresh mint leaves
2 tablespoons chopped fresh dill weed
2 tablespoons chopped fresh opal basil
2 cups assorted fresh flower blossoms
3 tablespoons chopped chives
1 watermelon radish, thinly sliced
watermelon vinaigrette
2 tablespoons toasted almond slivers
3 tablespoons white raisins
2 tablespoons sunflower seeds
2 tablespoons feta crumbles

Lightly toss all the greens, herbs, flowers, and the radish slices.

Pour desired amount of the vinaigrette in the bottom of two serving bowls.

Top with the salad mixture; this way the dressing will not make the delicate petals wilt and stick together.

Sprinkle with the almond slivers, raisins, sunflower seeds, and feta.

Serves 8

watermelon vinaigrette

3 cups watermelon chunks
½ cup olive oil
½ cup sherry vinegar
juice and zest of 1 lemon
1 teaspoon crushed pink peppercorns
1 teaspoon garlic salt

Liquify the watermelon in a food processor.

Whisk the oil, vinegar, lemon juice, zest and spices together, gradually add to the watermelon until well blended.

Makes 2 ½ cups

marigold cheese soup

6 tablespoons butter
1 white onion, minced
2 stalks celery, minced
2 carrots, minced
2 tablespoons flour
½ teaspoon dry mustard
1 quart chicken or vegetable broth
4 ounces brie, sliced
4 ounces shredded swiss
4 ounces shredded cheddar
1 cup heavy cream
½ cup marigold petals
Salt and pepper

Melt the butter in a large stockpot and sauté the vegetables until soft.

Stir in the flour and dry mustard, cooking for another 2 minutes while continuously stirring.

Gradually add the broth and bring to a boil.

Lower the heat, fold in the cheese, and stir until melted.

Add the cream and marigolds and continue to cook to desired consistency; do not allow to boil.

Salt and pepper to your taste.

Serves 6

wilted dandelion salad

4 slices thick-cut bacon, diced
2 cloves garlic, chopped
1 teaspoon dry mustard
1 tablespoon mustard seed
½ teaspoon celery salt
1 teaspoon cracked black pepper
2 tablespoons honey or maple syrup
5 tablespoons apple cider vinegar
4 cups dandelion greens
3 dozen dandelion blossoms
1 cup croutons
2 soft-boiled eggs

In a small saucepan, fry the bacon until crispy; remove the bacon pieces for later use.

Keeping all the fat in the pan, add the garlic, mustards, celery salt, pepper, honey, and vinegar.

Bring to a boil, stir in the bacon, and take off heat.

Immediately pour over the greens and flowers, and toss.

Top with croutons and place the egg in the center, sliced open to allow the yolk to ooze out.

Serves 4

33

Chapter Three

expanding my horizons

deli and bakery experience...

The desire to learn all I could about food had been sparked. As much as I loved my shop, in order to grow, I had to get out in the world and obtain more hands-on experience. I had some previous experience, helping with Friday-night fish fries and working at a truck stop diner while in high school, but now it was time to delve deep.

I was immediately hired by a local deli, where my obsession for cheese and charcuterie began. They allowed me to also spend time in the bakery, where I enjoyed baking bread but learned that while I found jelly-filled donuts to be delicious, I did not have a love for the process of making them. I continued to hold down these day jobs while working part-time nights at a restaurant . . . until I heard about the classes being offered at the Chippewa Valley Technical College in Eau Claire.

going after an associate degree in restaurant management...

I was fortunate to be awarded multiple scholarships, so I was soon on my way to attaining an associate degree in restaurant management. I enjoyed being in a classroom situation more than I'd expected. It certainly was a departure from the norm. I ended up graduating with honors, proud to carry a 4.0 GPA.

culinary competition...

During this time of formal education, I not only honed my God-given talents, but gained the confidence I needed to step out of my comfort zone. Not a person to partake in rivalry, I found myself in the frightening position of winning the opportunity to participate in the Wisconsin Restaurant Associations Student Culinary Competition. The requirements were to submit a luncheon entrée with one or two vegetables in an aspic glaze.

I labored over what dish to present. The application of aspic eliminated the use of my specialty, rich sauces. Having grown up at a fishing resort, I knew I would feel comfortable dealing with that style of protein. At the time, New Zealand was in the middle of a huge marketing campaign to help Americans fall in love with orange roughy. I knew that its meat would hold up well after cooking, and the white flesh would be a great backdrop for strategically placed herbs. My decision had been made: I would prepare poached orange roughy with zucchini and rissole potatoes.

> ### Rissole
> Rissole is a French cooking technique where partially cooked potatoes or potato patties are sauteed in butter and chives until golden brown. Most times the potato is peeled for a crunchy outside and creamy center.

The day before the competition, all the ingredients were gathered and packed in a cooler, ready for the four-hour road trip. Along the way, I read my recipe repeatedly, thinking of all the logistics involved. I felt calm and ready to do it . . . until I checked into the hotel.

I spent the evening in my room, doing any prep I could beforehand. Using a hot plate, I practiced by making miniature versions of the dish. Everything went well except the aspic application. Aspic is often used to glaze food pieces in food competitions. It protects the food from the air and makes it glisten for a fancier presentation. It can also be frustrating to work with, as I found out. I continued to have air bubbles form and an uneven coating, which would result in a deduction of points. After hours of trying different temperatures, adjusting the pace of pouring it, reducing the cooking fats on the potatoes, I finally had a perfect plate.

I managed to get a few hours of sleep before we were whisked off to let the games begin. With steady hands and the help of a hot needle, my dishes were near to perfection. With nothing left to do but await the judge's decision, I walked the floors of the showroom along with dozens of other nervous chefs. When the call came over the intercom for all competitors to gather, suddenly I lost my breath and my stomach gurgled with anticipation.

The presenter's words seemed garbled as he thanked the sponsors and explained their criteria for evaluation. All plates had been judged on appearance, craftsmanship, difficulty, originality, and food combinations. The honorable mentions were announced, and my name was not called. I had a sick disappointment, thinking that this was where I would fall, but the three top prizes were still left.

"The winner of the bronze medal is a first-year student who has impressed us not only with her capabilities, but also with her enthusiasm for the industry. Congratulations, Laurel..."

The world stood still for a moment. The person to my left patted me on the back. I found myself bounding out of my seat, jumping directly onto the stage, ignoring the stairs completely. When the presenter draped the medal around my neck, tears of excitement fell. At that moment I felt I had now gained the assuredness I would need to further my career.

Despite all my searching, I could not find my original recipe from the competition, so I thought I would share another similar dish I've made from the same ingredients.

poached orange roughy with sauteed vegetables

3 oranges, quartered
2 cups fish stock
1 cup non-oaked chardonnay
6 tablespoons butter
4 (6-ounce) orange roughy filets
1 teaspoon himalayan pink sea salt
1 tablespoon crushed pink peppercorns
2 fennel bulbs, sliced, save some fronds for garnish
1 red onion, cut in wedges
12 baby red potatoes, pre-cooked, quartered
2 medium zucchinis, thickly sliced
2 tablespoons chopped fresh oregano
1 tablespoon chopped garlic

In a large skillet, squeeze the juice from the oranges, straining out any seeds, and throw in the rinds.

Add stock, wine, and butter, bring to a boil.

Add the fish filets, sprinkle with salt and peppercorns, then reduce heat to a low simmer.

Depending how thick the filet is, simmer until the fish flakes easily, 8–10 minutes.

At the same time, in another large skillet, sauté the fennel, onion, potatoes, and zucchini in olive oil, and when almost done, toss in fresh oregano and garlic.

To serve, place a layer of the vegetable mixture in a dish with a wide slotted spatula, then remove the fish and place it on top of the vegetables in the middle of the dish. Turn flame up to high to reduce the poaching liquid, then ladle some over the top of the fish and garnish with the saved fennel fronds.

Serves 4

restaurant experience...

I worked for several years at a couple of Chippewa Falls' best restaurants. One of my favorites was called the Fill Inn Station. The Horstman family had converted the old Blue Diamond Gas Station into a cozy bar, restaurant, and banquet hall. It was here that I elevated my serving skills, winning "Waitperson of the Month" for six months in a row. It appeared that I was suddenly embracing that new competitive spirit!

They allowed me the opportunity to learn all aspects of the restaurant business. Along with serving, I was also a hostess and set up the salad bar/dessert tables.

True to Wisconsin tradition, they hosted a Friday night buffet, where I prepared the fresh fish. I would return to that same spot at the end of the line for Sunday brunch, flipping made-to-order omelets.

As much as I loved being around the customers, there was a special satisfaction that working in the kitchen offered. My shifts in the back, whether prepping or working the line, were a balancing factor in my life. When in the dining room, you were always performing, being a people pleaser. But in the kitchen, it was more of a sense of self-gratification. You concentrated on the chores at hand, your thoughts centered on one thing: putting out a tasty, appetizing plate of food.

Whether I was working in the front or the back of the house, I enjoyed my time there. It was a very efficient crew. And, like any good small-town restaurant, they had regular customers that treated the staff like family. How could I ever forget brothers Fred and Bill, two of the most loyal of patrons. I will always be grateful for the extra care they offered me during a time of personal crisis.

The restaurant must have been doing something right, they are still open to this day. It is now owned by Linda, our manager at the time. She is the gal in the middle of the picture with the green striped shirt.

One of the items that made this restaurant famous was their cheese curds. Honestly, I have yet to find any other as good as theirs. The recipe was secret; I don't recall anyone prepping them other than family members. The curd was large, resulting in a squeaky center with a gooey, stretchy outer layer. The beer batter coating was salty, yet sour. Using Leinenkugel's beer, from the brewery less than a mile away, must have been the secret ingredient.

I have tried to recreate them, but it is difficult to find curds that size. The following recipe is pretty darn close. Don't be surprised by the thin batter; you want it to just stick to the cheese, not form a fritter.

beer-battered cheese curds

1 pound fresh cheddar cheese curds, separated
2 eggs
1 teaspoon olive oil
3 tablespoons heavy cream
1 cup Leinenkugel's lager
1 cup flour, plus extra for coating
¼ teaspoon sea salt
1 teaspoon baking soda
2 quarts canola oil

Hint: Curds need to be consumed within a week or the squeak disappears, and they turn dry and salty.

Put your cheese curds in the freezer for an hour before cooking.

In a bowl beat the egg, olive oil, cream, and beer.

Add the flour, salt, and baking soda, mix until just blended.

Toss your frozen cheese curds in the extra flour so they are lightly coated, dip the curds in batter, and turn them to coat thoroughly.

Drop the coated curds into preheated 375-degree canola oil, a few at a time so they don't stick together.

Fry until golden brown and puffy, a couple of minutes; do not overcook or the cheese curd will burst through the batter.

Remove from oil and drain on paper towels.

Serves 6

The years of experience I gained here was priceless, but once again, it was time to move on to something different. I got the chance to cook and run the kitchen at the Elks Country Club kitchen for a season. Later, I went to the Chippewa Valley Regional Airport bar and restaurant overlooking the runway. Lynn McDonough, owner of the famed Connell's Supper Club, ran the place as Connell's II.

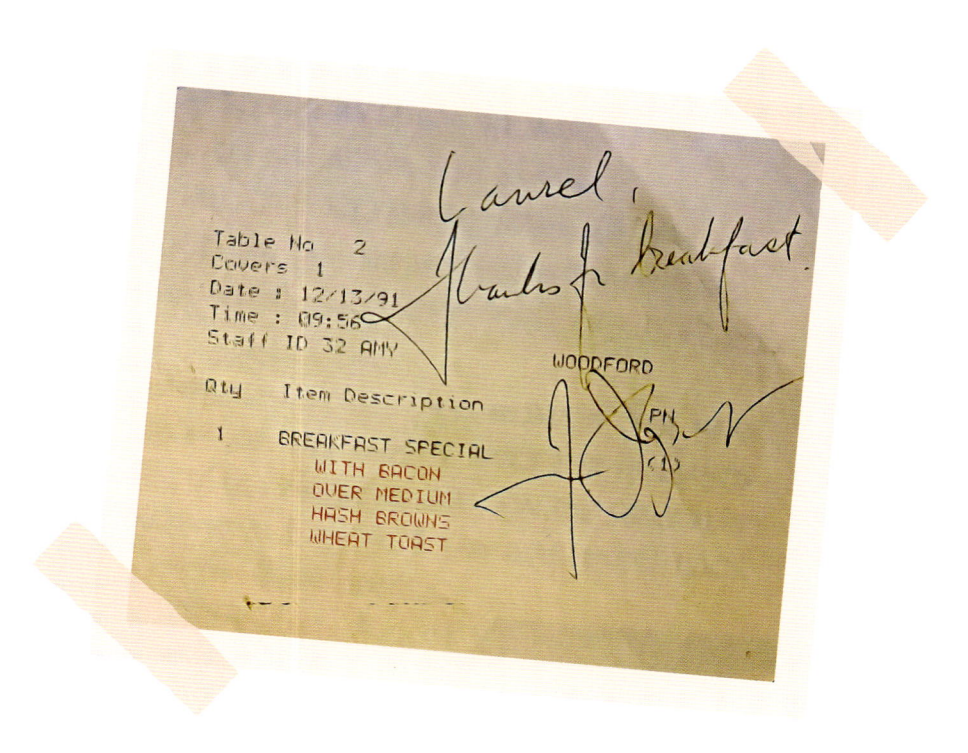

It was an honor working for him. He genuinely cared for his employees and did whatever he could to push you into improving yourself. For example, I did not like cooking breakfast; the darned eggs frustrated me. He knew this and continued to schedule me on that shift until I finally figured out the tricks to cooking a proper egg without throwing little temper tantrums. Two good things came out of this. I conquered a new skill, and in doing so, I got promoted. And I got to cook breakfast for Tom Wopat, Luke Duke from the Dukes of Hazzard show!

Wisconsin had given me just over thirty years of education and memories. I had experienced some of the best moments of my life and some of the worst. As much as I loved this state that I had called home, it was time to uproot. Maybe it was watching the planes fly in and out every day, perhaps it was just time to start a new phase of my life, but I was struck with wanderlust.

One of the bartenders had attended college in Sioux Falls, South Dakota and always talked highly about it, so we decided to take a road trip to check it out. I fell in love with the growing town, seeing the opportunities it could offer me. While sitting in the Crow Bar, the city's iconic dive bar, I made the decision to move. I said my good-byes to Chippewa Falls and ventured onto the plains of South Dakota.

Chapter Four

time to step into management

sioux falls brewing company...

I would take strolls through the downtown area, admiring the old pink quartzite buildings. Though unique from the limestone structures of Wisconsin, they somehow helped to ease my homesickness. The area was suffering from urban decay. Empty storefronts called out as I would pass by, yearning for someone to bring them back to their glory. Grandiose ideas ran through my mind as I headed north on Phillips Avenue. I knew the timing wasn't quite right for the release of my entrepreneurial desires, but I definitely wanted to be a part of the downtown's revival.

My daydreams were interrupted by the sounds of construction. A whiff of sawdust and curiosity lured me into a four-story building that was undergoing renovations. The first floor was abuzz with workers. I was sent to a second-floor office to get all my questions answered. Little did I know that this conversation was going to lead to a job that I would devote the next five years to and where I would develop lifelong friendships.

This grand building was originally the Jewett Brothers Warehouse built in 1899, which stored dry goods, food, and medicine. In 1927 the family retired and sold it to their competitors, Nash Finch Wholesalers. The new owners, Koch Hazard Baltzer Architects, were finishing restoration of the newly named Falls Center. Their offices, along with others, were located on the second floor.

My new employer, The Sioux Falls Brewing Company, was renovating the main floor and lower level. This location was just a few blocks away from the original Sioux Falls Brewing and Malting Company that opened in 1898. By starting this business, they would be bringing back the brewing tradition to this town. Many people doubted their decision to put so much work into a building that was located in an area called the "no-man's-land," but their vision helped to start the area's recovery.

Most restaurants and bars are the result of someone's passion, and this was no different. Dean Stalheim and Dan Zaayer had been home brewers for years. Friends kept telling them that they needed to start their own business. When one of Dean's friends introduced him to Mike Pospischil, who was a successful restaurateur, the venture began.

It was exciting to watch the progress as Swift Contractors steadily labored to complete all the work before the opening date. To watch the menu come together and see the brewers creating their beers, all amid the chaos, was exhilarating. I was looking for a new experience and this was definitely going to fit the bill. Not only was this the first restaurant where I was a part of the birth, but also the largest one I'd worked in. The front dining room sat 150 guests, the pub area 175, and the patio had room for another 150. As hostess, I knew that I was going to put in a lot of miles.

The saying "if you build it, they will come" was proven true by the overwhelming response upon opening early in 1995. The wide expanse of scarred wooden floors filled in quickly. This was an energy that would continue day after day. Pints of handcrafted beers were being tapped as fast as the bartenders could pull. They started with four beers: Prairie Wheat, Phillips Avenue Pale Ale, Buffalo Stout, and the biggest seller, Ringneck Red. Despite the lite beer trend, the full-flavored ales were being embraced. The brewers began creating unique specialty brews to appease the adventurous drinkers. By the end of the first year in business, they would have produced over sixteen hundred barrels.

The kitchen sent out plate after plate, always a wave of tickets on the line. Buffalo burgers and the homemade sausages were favorites, however what made the menu so unique at that time was the use of beer as an actual ingredient. I had always cooked with wine, so seeing recipes converted over with a malty edge was intriguing to me and our customers. Chef Rod fried shrimp that had been rolled in barley and coconut and created a creamy, decadent stout cheesecake. We even tried making bread with the spent grain, but the consistency just didn't hold up. Ultimately, the grain was sent to a cattle farmer and the cows loved it. The farmer told us that when the cows saw the truck coming with the grain, they would run to greet the driver!

We had a lot of dishes that stood out from any other menu in town. One of my personal favorites was the t-rex wings. The turkey wings were brought in from a farm up north. Big and spicy, you couldn't help ending up with a face full of sauce and a sweaty forehead from the heat. Consumption of beer certainly soared while battling this dish. If Casey Webb had had his Travel Channel show, Man v. Food, back then, this would have brought him to Sioux Falls.

T-rex Wings $5.95
a house specialty sure to satisfy the biggest & meanest appetite. Celery sticks and ranch dressing accompany the platter.

t-rex wings

4 pounds turkey wings and drummies, bone-in, skin-on
¼ cup olive oil
3 tablespoons thyme
salt and pepper to taste
beer
t-rex sauce

Rub the turkey with the oil and spices, place on a baking sheet, pour enough beer just to build a little steam, and wrap tightly with foil.

Bake at 400 degrees for 1 full hour or until meat temps to 160 degrees.

Let sit for 10 minutes before removing foil.

If ready to serve immediately, dip in the sauce and enjoy.

If not used right away, refrigerate until ready to serve.

We dipped them in the fryer to reheat, but because of their size you may need to reheat the in the oven, wrapped in foil.

Serves 8

t-rex sauce

2 tablespoons instant coffee granules
¼ cup liquid smoke
7¾ cups ketchup
2 tablespoons yellow mustard
¼ cup cajun spice
1 onion, finely minced
¼ cup minced garlic
1 tablespoon worcestershire sauce
1 pound brown sugar
¾ pound white sugar
1½ cups cider vinegar
5 teaspoons Tabasco sauce
½ cup chili powder

Simmer all the ingredients for half an hour.

Makes 3 pints

event planning...

In less than a year, I was promoted to the manager's position. Along with the restaurant duties, I also became an event planner. I worked side-by-side with Mike, sitting in our office for hours bouncing ideas off each other. The partnership between Mike and me was magical. From brewmaster or wine dinners, to concerts and charitable fundraisers, we weren't afraid to attempt something new . . . and everything we tried worked!

One of the earliest events was a charitable chili cook-off. Some memories tend to fade as the years pass, but I do recall the excitement of this day. The turnout for competitors and tasters was high. I even decided to enter!

The large room quickly filled in with tables full of Crock-Pots and a tangle of extension cords. Guests could purchase tickets and wander through the array of chili, tasting each recipe with a cold beer in hand. They would drop a ticket in the bucket next to the pot they thought was the best. Each ticket counted as a vote.

As the official judges discussed among themselves and counted the votes, all of us competitors gathered to try each other's chili. The aroma of spice and corn chips was heavy on our breath as we exchanged the "secret" ingredients that would make ours the winning recipe. They finally announced the winner—darn, not me, but the disappointment didn't last for long. I won the people's choice! That was even better! The judges liked a very spicy, more traditional, no-bean recipe, but my peers loved the rich, deep flavor that the unexpected peanut butter and chocolate brought to my smoky peppers. Give my recipe a try and see what you think!

spicy garden pepper chili

½ pound ground beef
½ pound chorizo
2 green bell peppers, diced
2 red bell peppers, diced
1 jalapeño, thinly sliced
1 poblano, diced
2 yellow onions, diced
6 cloves garlic, minced
2½ pounds tomatoes, diced
1 tablespoon chili garlic sauce
1 tablespoon chipotle paste
1 (28-ounce) can tomato sauce
¼ cup peanut butter
2 tablespoons ground cumin
2 tablespoons chili powder
½ tablespoon thyme
½ tablespoon crushed pink peppercorns
1 tablespoon sea salt
1 dried arbol chili, crushed
2 dried morita chili, crushed
2 tablespoon grated dark chocolate
1 (16-ounce) can lager
1 (16-ounce) canned red beans, drain fluid
grated cheese or sour cream for garnish

In a large pot, brown the ground beef and chorizo.

Add the fresh peppers, onion, and garlic, cook until the onions are translucent.

Add the tomatoes, chili garlic sauce, chipotle paste, tomato sauce, and peanut butter. Stir until blended.

Add the spices, dried chilis, and chocolate.

Once the chocolate has melted, add the beer and beans. Allow to slow simmer for at least two hours, so flavors can meld. Add water to thin out if you prefer a "brothier" chili.

Garnish with grated cheese or a dollop of sour cream.

Serves 8

The next four years were a whirlwind. Sometimes I laughingly shake my head and wonder how I survived it all. I lived and loved the Sioux Falls Brewing Company. There were so many memorable occasions that I was proud to be a part of.

One of the most romantic would have to be the Jim Brickman concert. For those not familiar with him, he is a Grammy-nominated songwriter, performer, and world-class pianist.

We set the south lot with rows of round tables draped in crisp linens and illuminated with candles. His white baby grand piano was elevated on the deck, with the backdrop of the Courthouse Museum clock tower and an almost full moon. It was a beautiful starry night for dining al fresco. Everything about that evening was picturesque.

We hosted gatherings to excite all personalities. Dick Dale, the pioneer of surf music, rocked our lower-level bar named the Cavern Tavern. On the patio, everyone jammed along with Billy Bacon and the Forbidden Pigs' rockabilly music and sang the blues with diva Candye Kane, who wrote songs of self-acceptance and championed for the LGBT community.

52

Supporting the arts, along with the South Dakota Public Broadcasting Station, we had Canadian legend Red Green make us all laugh and teach us home improvement skills using duct tape. Working with the film society, the outer wall of the food pantry was painted with a stage curtain where they projected classic movies. This outdoor theater was supported by fans who brought their own couches, beach chairs, and loungers.

hot harley nights...

The event I am most proud of is Hot Harley Nights. When Jim Entenman, owner of J&L Harley-Davidson, approached us about wanting to host a fundraiser for Make-A-Wish, we were happy to oblige. After weeks of meetings, the event was officially created. After a day of exploring the town during a poker run, they would gather at J&L's and parade together to the brewpub. There we would feed the hungry bikers while listening to live music.

Since we would be going through all the work to assemble a stage and set up outdoor bars, the decision was made to also host a concert the night before. Margarita and beer booths welcomed the parrot heads that came to dance the night away to A1A, the official Jimmy Buffett tribute band. To accommodate all the additional revelers, we needed to enlist some extra hands. Terry & Lynette Kelley and Pete & Paula Vogelsang volunteered to be the official cocktail shakers and continued to do so every year.

The next day we would transition from bright Hawaiian shirts to black leather. We scurried to change over to Jack Daniel's booths and fill the grills with sausages. After months of planning, it was exciting to see it all come together. All the staff were on duty manning stations inside and out.

Meanwhile at J&L's, everyone was returning from the poker run and getting ready to start the parade. I arrived just in time to jump on the back of a friend's bike as we began the route back to the brewpub. Hundreds of hogs made their way, revving their motors to cheering supporters. Once we entered the downtown area, the reverberation shook the windows. The tall buildings held in the echoes and the exhaust. It truly was a sensory experience hard to describe.

As the bikes parked, lining up for viewing, I rejoined the staff who were already hard at work, ready for another busy evening. The event raised over $3,000 that night. It continued to gain in popularity every year, eventually outgrowing the downtown area, with close to four thousand riders. Twenty-five years later, Hot Harley Nights has raised over $3 million to help grant the wishes of South Dakota children with critical illnesses. I am delighted to have been a sponsoring partner for the first five years, then continued to donate to the cause. In 2020 the event was canceled because of Covid restrictions, but it will return this year bigger and better than ever.

inspiration of carole pagones...

One of the influential people I met while at the brewpub was Carole Pagones. She was the executive director of Main Street Sioux Falls, leading the way for the revitalization of downtown. You would see her at every event and parade, working tirelessly to ensure its success. She walked the street, stopping in the shops to speak with the owners, keeping in touch with their needs or sharing new ideas.

I was fortunate to work on committees with Carole, where she taught me community pride and made me realize that it was okay to aspire to greater achievements. Thanks to her confidence in me, I realized that the time had come to leave the comfort of my job and start my own business again.

Carole continued to check in on me throughout my career moves! Unfortunately, she just recently passed away. I had hoped to see the surprised look on her face as she perused this book. I do know that she would have been proud! Our cranberry turkey was her favorite sandwich, she said the flavors reminded her of Thanksgiving, leaving that feeling of just enjoying a feast. While she was ailing a driver would be sent to pick one up for her. I hope there was one waiting for her up there in heaven…

Chapter Five

getting back to entrepreneurism

food n' fermentations...

The backyard deck at home is my "think tank"; many great ideas have been hatched while watching the birds and squirrels play there. One night, after opening a bottle of cabernet, my fiance, Doug, and I had settled into the chairs enjoying the brisk late summer breeze. He must have known something was up since I hadn't come out with my usual stack of magazines. I jumped right into it, announcing that I was going in tomorrow to put in my two weeks' notice and was going to open my own store. He was surprisingly supportive about it. As you can imagine, we conversed for hours planning out how our new life was going to unfold.

The next morning, I woke up feeling excited, yet feelings of trepidation also lay heavy as scenarios of me quitting ran through my mind. I finished my coffee and strolled down the pathway to my car. I took in a big breath of air and turned the key in the ignition. The radio blasted the news, the reporter's voice breaking from anxiety. What do you mean, something hit one of the Twin Towers?! I drove slowly, listening to every word in disbelief. I arrived to find stunned employees gathered around the television.

We all know how the events of this horrific day unfolded. Dealing with customers that ranged from angry to bewildered was a daunting task. The security that we had taken for granted had been instantaneously shattered. Suddenly, my decision to become an entrepreneur appeared to be a precarious one.

After another fireside chat, Doug and I agreed that now more than ever we needed to have faith in our country. For stability, Doug would remain in his job as bartender at Theo's, but I would begin my search for a storefront. To lessen the risk, I resolved to be a wine and gourmet food shop and not a restaurant. Carole, excited to get me downtown, assisted in finding the building that would work for my vision.

With plenty of options available at the time, I finally decided on the old Michael's and Burke's building at 222 S. Phillips Ave. The clothing store had opened as Burke's in 1954, and shortly thereafter they opened Michael's next door. With an indoor opening adjoining the two locations, it provided an easy opportunity for future expansion.

I wasted no time filling the fifteen hundred square feet with a selection of over five hundred wines and an impressive collection of scotch and unique liqueurs. There were coolers full of cheese and charcuterie from all over the world. Specialty food and wine accessories were displayed on various pieces of antique furniture.

With everything in its place, we opened the doors to introduce Food n' Fermentations, on December 7, 2001.

surfsUp partnership...

A year later, business was good, and thanks to my sales reps, my knowledge of wine was growing in leaps and bounds. I was getting plenty of press, bringing in even more adventurous customers. I didn't think it could get any better, then I got the exciting news that I was going to have a neighbor in the adjoining space. The Sioux Falls Brewing Company had closed, and Mike, along with his wife, Barb, were going to open a seafood restaurant next door, called SurfsUp. The dynamic duo was going to be working together again!

With the doors wide open, customers flowed between our places. A lot of our shoppers ended up dining there, lured by the aromas coming from their kitchen. We were the fun place to peruse while their guests waited for a table. One could also purchase a bottle of wine and take it over to enjoy along with their dinner. There were no two places with a more perfect partnership than the one our businesses shared.

Food n' Fermentations had a wicker table and chairs in the front of the store where the sun shone through. A pile of trade magazines and my notes from wine tastings with the reps sat ready for research. When the fresh seafood came in at SurfsUp, Mike would prepare a dish and we would sit there nibbling and sipping wines to find the perfect pairing. It was at that table where I was truly educated about all the delicacies that come from the sea.

I would never be forgiven if I didn't share some recipes for oysters with you. They are Doug's favorite shellfish. People either love them or hate them. Whether you enjoy slurping oysters raw or prefer them cooked, they are highly nutritious, packed with protein, vitamins, minerals, and antioxidants. They are extremely rich in zinc, which boosts your testosterone, increasing libido. This aphrodisiac effect is increased by the experience of eating them. The feel of the oyster in your mouth and the taste of the salty juices can be genuinely arousing. Enjoy with a glass of chablis, champagne, absinthe, or a dirty martini and you're on your way to a carnal adventure.

There are over two hundred unique varieties. Much like a wine, each one is distinctly different from the others due to terroir or, in the oyster world, merroir. "Mer" is French for sea, so the term merroir is used to describe how a particular area's climate and soil will affect the taste of seafood, most specifically used for oysters. The delicate flesh takes on the flavor of the waters in which the oysters grow. Each kind has a different shell coloring and shape. Having a basic knowledge of the varieties when shopping just might help turn haters into believers.

Atlantic oysters are found along the east coast, from Canada down to the Gulf of Mexico. They tend to be larger, and full of rich, salty brine. The meat is plump, with a crisp minerality and clean finish. The most common varieties are Virginica, Blue Point, Chesapeake Bay, and Wellfleet.

The strongest tasting oyster, the European Flat, also comes from this area. You need to be a true oyster lover to enjoy them. They are meaty, with an intense seaweed flavor and a strong metallic finish. The large Belon oyster was brought to Maine from France in the 1950s. Just as Kobe beef is Wagyu, but not all Wagyu is Kobe, so it goes with Belons. Belons are European Flats, but not all European Flats are Belons. They must be harvested from the Belon River in the Brittany region of France.

Pacific oysters are not native to the area, except for one variety, the Olympia. They were so popular that by the end of the 1800s they were wiped out and thought to be extinct. Oysters were then brought over from Asia to rebuild the beds. Years later, however, a few Olympias were found in the Pacific Northwest, and they are now being farmed in small numbers in British Columbia and Puget Sound. They are usually smaller in size and have a west coast complexity in their flavor, ranging from grassy and herbaceous to fruity melon. The brine is milder, with a cucumber freshness. The most common varieties are Kumamoto and Miyagi, Kumo, Penn Cove Select, Fanny Bay, and Kusshi.

Gulf Coast oysters are basically the same as Atlantic varieties but harvested along the coast of Florida, Alabama, Mississippi, Louisiana, and Texas. Because the water temperatures get too warm and the oysters spawn, you do not want to eat them fresh from this region between May through August. In the other months though, they are meaty yet tender, with a mild sweetness. Many inland restaurants use AmeriPure oysters from the Gulf of Mexico. The Louisiana-owned company sells over 20 million oysters yearly. Their patented water-bath process removes potentially harmful bacteria to non-detectable levels, basically pasteurizing the oysters, to make them safe to eat raw.

oysters rockefeller

2 tablespoons butter
12 ounces baby spinach
2 green onions, white part only, finely minced
1 tablespoon garlic, minced
24 oysters on the half shell
½ cup grated gruyère

In a sauté pan, melt the butter, then add the spinach, onion, and garlic, and cook until the spinach is wilted. Drain any extra liquid.

Spoon the mixture on top of the oysters. Top with grated cheese.

Broil or grill until the topping is bubbling and golden brown. Do not overcook!

Serve the oysters on a bed of rock salt with lemon slices.

Serves 6

Rockefeller Origins

Jules Alciatore from Antoine's Restaurant in New Orleans, Louisiana is known as the first chef to make Oysters Rockefeller. According to legend, while enjoying the oysters a customer exclaimed with glee, "Why, this is as rich as Rockefeller!" Since they were the color of greenbacks and as opulent as John D. Rockefeller, the recipe was so named.

honey cajun grilled oysters

1 dozen oysters on the half shell
4 tablespoons butter
2 tablespoons honey
cajun seasoning

On each oyster, place a dollop of butter, generously drizzle with honey, and add a healthy dash of spice.

Put on a char grill and cook just until the fluid bubbles.

Serves 4

caprese oysters

1 tablespoon butter
2 ounces fresh basil
6 ounces baby spinach, chopped
1 tablespoon garlic, minced
24 oysters on the half shell
4 small tomatoes, thinly sliced
8 ounces fresh mozzarella, torn in small pieces
1/4 cup grated parmigiano reggiano
balsamic glaze

In a sauté pan, melt the butter and add the basil, spinach, and garlic; cook until the spinach is just wilted.

Drain any extra liquid. Spoon the mixture on top of the oysters.

Top each oyster with a tomato slice, mozzarella, then parmigiano.

Broil or grill until the topping is bubbling and golden brown. Do not overcook!

Garnish with a light drizzle of balsamic.

Serves 6

oysters with mignonette

2 dozen oysters on the half shelf
½ cup red wine vinegar
2 tablespoons finely minced red onion
3 tablespoons finely minced chives
½ teaspoon grated horseradish
½ teaspoon lemon juice
½ teaspoon salt

Mix all the ingredients well. Chill for 1 hour to let flavors meld. Spoon on oysters once served.

Serves 6

Hint: Don't throw away your oyster shells, put them in your garden or potted plants. The calcium in the shells will help your flowers be stronger and have brighter colors . . . and the squirrels chew on them to sharpen their teeth!

oyster and sea asparagus chowder

3 dozen oysters, shucked, all liquor reserved
3 tablespoons unsalted butter
1 leek, white part only, sliced
1 tablespoon minced garlic
6 cups fish stock or clam broth
3 potatoes, finely chopped
2 cups heavy cream
3 ounces sea asparagus, chopped
1 teaspoon lemon pepper
salt and pepper to taste

Shuck the oysters and reserve the liquor.

Melt the butter in a stockpot, then sauté the leek and garlic until softened.

Add the broth and potatoes, cover, and simmer until the potatoes are cooked through.

Add the heavy cream, sea asparagus, and lemon pepper.

Simmer for 15 minutes. Add the oysters and their liquor.

Salt and pepper to taste, cook for another 5 minutes.

Serve with crackers. We brushed saltines with melted butter mixed with old bay seasoning.

Serves 8 - 10

> Hint: Sea asparagus is a succulent that grows in salt marshes, on beaches, and among mangroves. It's a superfood, high in vitamins and nutrients, with a crispy texture and salty flavor.

changing laws of downtown...

The downtown area was all abuzz about the plans to extend Phillips Avenue north to our city's namesake at Falls Park. Developers and investors were making major improvements to the area. Upper levels of buildings were now being turned into lofts and offices. People were feeling more comfortable walking the streets. It was an exciting time.

After a long battle, the infamous "Loop" was shut down. Without the constant cruising of vehicles, the teens and young adults didn't congregate on the street corners and parking lots at night. This created the opportunity for businesses to stay open later and to begin having outdoor dining.

All of these changes kicked my creative wheels in gear, and I began to envision an all-new version of Food n' Fermentations. The idea of having both a retail shop and a restaurant, all in one space, rolled through my mind. The only problem was licensing. At the time, you could not sell and serve in the same location. There would also be issues with consumption on outdoor property that was not an attached patio. We would have to put tables on the brick curb extensions that were city property.

After I expressed my dilemma to Carole, she set up a meeting with influential people who could help solve my growth problems. I was honored to sit down to dinner with US State Senator Tom Daschle and other influencers who wanted not only to assist me, but to help all business owners, present and in the future.

Eventually, the laws were changed, Phillips Avenue was extended all the way to the falls, and a portal to downtown was opened for tourists. The newly established outdoor Sculpture Walk exhibit brought more attention to the freshly groomed area, and empty storefronts were filling in quickly.

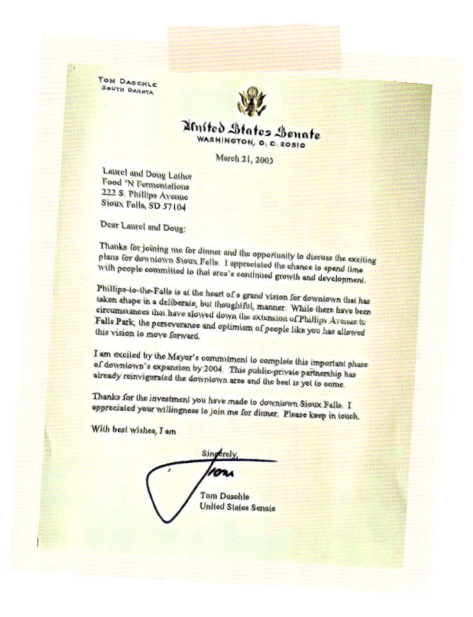

When I was told that the owner of the Phillips Avenue Bakery was retiring, I knew this was the place meant for me. As much as I hated to break up the business relationship I had with Mike, my yearning to get back to the kitchen was strong. If I didn't take advantage of this opportunity, it might not present itself again.

After a heartfelt conversation with my SurfsUp buddy, I signed the lease to a new beginning. With a lot of help from friends and supporters everything was moved from 222 to 212 S. Phillips.

Chapter Six

time to put the chef's coat back on

food n' fermentations II...

The dark wood and brick walls had an old-world charm that would contribute to the warmth you felt when walking through the doors. A wide staircase led to the wine cellar and liquor library on the lower level. The original wood floors guided you to the roomy booths, which were handmade by a local artisan from an old ash tree that had stood next to the Klondike Mill, now a ghost town. They would soon become a haven for single diners in the afternoon, who would curl up and enjoy a cheese plate, read the news, or catch up on paperwork. My favorite spot was the round family table in the sunny front window.

I spent hours moving furniture back and forth, setting up my kitchen, just taking in the personality of the building. As I did this, memories of our trip to wine country kept surfacing. One of our favorite experiences was at V. Sattui, not only an award-winning winery, but also an upscale grocery that offered every delectable cheese and charcuterie you could wish for. You could select a bottle of wine, loaf of bread, and olives, then go outside to picnic under the giant oak trees. This would be my inspiration for the menu. "Napa Valley grazing" became our theme.

After you'd shopped from the deli to create your own picnic, we'd gladly give you a cutting board and help set you up at your table. You could also give us your budget and specific tastes and we would create a board from our selection of well over a hundred cheeses and charcuterie. We had all the accompaniments: nuts, olives, fruit, preserves, and mustards. Customers could try something new every day if they wanted to.

Along with the cheese board, many would order our house-made soups. This was my specialty; I made a different soup every week, but we always had the chianti tomato basil. Its popularity continued for years to come. We saved the wicker chianti bottles used for this soup to decorate the beams, and later filled an entire wall with them. When I asked on Facebook which recipes I should put in my book, this was the most requested!

chianti tomato basil soup

4 pounds fresh tomatoes or 6 cups canned diced tomatoes
2 tablespoons minced garlic
4 ounces fresh basil, chopped
6 cups tomato sauce
6 cups water
½ bottle (750 milliliters) chianti
¼ cup fennel seed
½ tablespoon sea salt
4 ounces parmigiano reggiano (purchase with rind if possible)

Chop the tomatoes, garlic, and basil.

Put the tomatoes, tomato sauce, water, and chianti in a stockpot.

Add the basil, fennel, garlic, and salt.

Cut the rind off the parmigiano and put it in the

soup (if rind is not available, use 2 ounces of the cheese shredded).

Bring to a boil, then simmer on low heat until flavors have melded together.

When serving, shave the remaining parmigiano on top. Serve with a grilled baguette.

Serves 10

With a wonderful array of fromage available, you can imagine the luscious macaroni and cheese we created. We had a base recipe that any little odds and ends could be thrown into. At times, there could be over eighteen varieties!

Chianti

Chianti is an expression of the sangiovese grape from Tuscany's rolling hills. Dating back to the fifteenth century, its popularity continued to soar. As the demand spread farther around the country, the cost of hauling heavy bottles rose. It was cheaper to make thin glass bottles with rounded bottoms rather than the standard 750ml bottle. To stabilize the base, they wrapped them in straw, which also protected the bottle during transportation. This is called a fiasco.

macNcheese

1½ pound macaroni
½ pound smoked gouda, grated, including brown rind
¼ pound brie, include the bloom rind if still snowy white
¼ pound taleggio
2 cups cheddar cheese sauce
2½ cups milk
6 green onions, small diced
¼ pound feta, crumbled
¼ pound fresh mozzarella, torn in pieces
¼ cup pepper supreme

Cook the macaroni in salted boiling water until al dente, drain, and rinse with cool water.

In a saucepan, melt the Gouda, Brie, taleggio, the cheddar cheese sauce and milk, stirring often until smooth.

Place the noodles in a large bowl. Pour the hot cheese sauce over them. Add pepper supreme, green onions, feta, and mozzarella, stirring gently. Add additional milk if needed.

Serves 8 - 10

While waiting for their cheese board to be put together or their meal to be cooked, many would saunter downstairs to the wine cellar. There were over six hundred wines from around the globe to select from. Utilizing the new law change, you could purchase any of them to take home or enjoy at your table. We were the first place in the state where you could buy a glass of wine and enjoy it while shopping.

If you were interested in expanding your wine knowledge, we were the place to go. The tasting bar was open on Saturdays for sampling, often hosted by winery reps or the winemakers themselves. There was also a comfy nook where you could sit in seats from the old State Theatre to watch informational DVDs about wine.

Our staff was also well trained, and excited to help you select the perfect wine-and-cheese pairing. They were all young, enthusiastic, and eager to learn as much as possible. Our sales reps helped nurture their passion. Anne Barnes, now Anne Barnes Koziara, VP of on-premise at Riedel Crystal of America, worked diligently with us. She is responsible for igniting my love for French wines. Tim Alick and Paul Nester, with me from back in the Sioux Falls Brewing Company days, continued to support and were a big part of special events.

Originally, we were only open during the day, closing at 6 p.m. We would host random special events in the evening. Our lunch hours were intense and high-spirited. Jackie and Jes, who's personalities were as colorful as their tattoos, were experts behind the sandwich counter. Eli and John's specialty was selling wine and cheese. This was one of my favorite teams. The core group was assisted by part-timers who brought much needed relief.

In one of our first restaurant reviews it was reported that "our server was charming and helpful, unfinished but with wine and food moxie that belied their youth." This showed how much the staff cared and how hard they worked and studied to be the best they could be.

Fresh & Satisfying Sandwiches
$3.95 Half $6.95 Whole

Mesquite Turkey – port salut cheese tames a sassy mesquite smoked turkey breast, pecan-cranberry sauce adds a perky lift inside wildrice cranberry bread.

Strawberry Ham – Ham from the Black Forest meets French brie cheese, mingles with fresh strawberries and welcomes a dash of stoneground mustard with strawberry preserves on a multigrain ciabatta roll.

Mini Beef Wellingtons – roasted beef, mushroom pate and thin sliced onion, accented by a dab of stoneground mustard, encased on petit sourdough buns with a side of burgundy au jus

Skipjack Boat – tuna, celery, scallions, capers, olives and dill are tossed in a light wave of olive oil & sauvignon blanc vinegar, then stuffed in a dug-out of foccacia bread

John's Egg Salad – the best of comfort foods; eggs, scallions and celery embraced with mayo and a hug of stoneground mustard, nestled on a romaine leaf on soft sourdough bread.

Jackie's Spring Roll – Bean sprouts, carrots, lettuce, fresh mint and tofu are delicately rolled in rice paper, served with a peanut sauce

Focaccia Torte $4.95 – Sorry, we can't do halves on this sandwich! genoa salami, capicolla, tomato, onion, roasted red pepper, black olives and provolone cheese are layered with basil pesto smothered focaccia.

Our sandwiches were hearty, with top-notch ingredients. The employees loved contributing their own versions. We had a couple of vegetarians who helped to balance the rib-stickin' meaty options on the menu. Jackie prepared delightfully refreshing spring rolls, and equally popular was the calabrese flatbread.

calabrese flatbread

1 eggplant, sliced lengthwise into 4 planks
olive oil
sea salt and pepper
8 ounces mozzarella, sliced
½ cup fresh basil, minced
2 tomatoes, sliced
4 naan or pita bread
¼ cup calabrese peppers in oil
spinach, chopped
balsamic glaze
pickled shredded carrot

Generously rub the eggplant slices with olive oil, season with salt and pepper, and grill or fry.

Once you flip to brown the other side, lay the mozzarella on top and cover with the basil, then the tomato slices.

Meanwhile, warm the naan and rub the top side with mashed calabrese peppers.

On half of the naan, lay down a bed of spinach and top with the eggplant that's been browned with the cheese, basil, and tomato.

Drizzle with balsamic glaze and olive oil, garnish with pickled carrots, fold over, and enjoy.

Serves 4

We baked a sourdough bread that was so light, we used it for the skipjack boat because it was easy to press into the shape of a dugout. Sliced thickly, it was also perfect for John's egg salad sandwich, which was described as deviled eggs between two heavenly clouds. And who doesn't love deviled eggs? With maybe the exception of stuffed peppadew peppers, they were the most requested finger food.

deviled eggs

6 eggs, hardboiled, peeled
5 tablespoons mayo
1 tablespoon horseradish
½ tablespoon dijon mustard
¾ teaspoon dill weed
¼ teaspoon garlic powder
salt to taste

Cut the eggs in half lengthwise, pop out the yolk into a bowl, and place the whites on a plate.

Add the remaining ingredients and mash with a fork, mixing until smooth.

Put the filling into a piping bag and portion evenly into the egg white shells.

Garnish as you like. You can be as creative as you want. As you can see, I loved trying all kinds of varieties. Here are some of my favorites:

Easter-themed eggs were topped with pastel-colored tobiko caviar, sprinkled with black sesame seeds, and tucked in sunflower micros.

For the kimchi eggs I substituted ⅛ teaspoon of wasabi for the dijon mustard, spooned a small amount of finely chopped kimchi on top, then sprinkled with black and wasabi sesame seeds.

The combo plate had a bacon-and-onion egg and a beet egg. For the bacon-and-onion eggs: substitute onion powder for the garlic powder and fresh chives for the dill weed, and garnish with crispy fried onion bits and crumbled bacon. For the beet eggs: substitute 2 tablespoons mashed cooked beets for 2 tablespoons of the mayo, omit the mustard, garnish with small diced beets and chopped chives, and sprinkle with celery seed.

The spring pea recipe substituted 1 tablespoon pea puree for 1 tablespoon mayo and ⅛ teaspoon wasabi for the dijon mustard, omitted the garlic powder, and topped the eggs with sweety drop pepper and pea shoots sprinkled with wasabi sesame seeds.

special events...

We loved hosting the bimonthly wine dinners, always coming up with a theme to carry throughout the evening. One of the most elaborate nights was when we had both floors set up as a French speakeasy. We blacked out the front window and locked the doors; entry could only be gained through the alley with a secret password. Tables were spread out representing the different French regions with the wines and food indigenous to each area.

The most popular event was the Annual Fish Fry. South Dakotans are known for their love of walleye, and no one more than my husband shares this passion. We fell in love on a Canadian fishing trip after surviving a deadly storm together. That didn't stop us from returning every year, getting back on those cold waters to catch the biggest of walleyes. After three years, we got married in 2001, on the dock after a great day of fishing. So every May we celebrate with a classic shore lunch.

Although a shore lunch is truly just a reason to take a break from the boat and enjoy your freshly caught fish, what makes it so special is the camaraderie of sharing your stories of the day. We looked forward to gathering with all our fishing buddies at the pink rock, a landmark rock formation on Lac Seul Lake. Years ago, someone took the time to build a fire pit that beckons to area anglers.

We all chip in on duties, from starting the fire, cleaning the fish, cooking and of course, the dreaded dish detail. Typically, we fried fish and taters, heated up beans, and enjoyed a cold brew.

For the annual fish fry event, Doug was the honorary fryer of the fish and would make his family's secret sauce for dipping. The rest of the meal was on me—taters and beans, but this time they're not cooked in the can. With cold beers and glasses of chardonnay in hand, our guests roamed about sharing their fish tales. We held a contest for the best fishing picture, so it was fun to see everyone's photos of fame.

Eventually walleye was no longer just an annual treat and found its place on the menu. The shore lunch sandwich was impressive, with the long filet hanging over the sides of the bun. These crispy edges were often broken off by the diner as a tasty tidbit before biting into the juicy, thick meat inside.

lemon peppered walleye sammie

2 (6-ounce) walleye filet
flour to coat filet
lemon pepper to season
canola oil
2 brioche bun, brushed with extra virgin olive oil and grilled
1/4 cup caper aioli
mixed spring greens
pickled red onions

Dredge the walleye filet in flour. Season both sides with lemon pepper. Fill a fry pan with about 1 inch of canola oil, and when hot, add the filet and cook until golden brown on both sides.

Spread 1 tablespoon of caper aioli on the bottom bun. Put down a bed of greens, then the walleye. Top with pickled red onion. Spread a tablespoon of caper aioli on the top bun.

Serves 2

pickled red onions

4 red onions
2 cups rice vinegar
2 cups water
1 cup sugar
2 tablespoons dill weed
1 tablespoon red pepper flakes
1 teaspoon sea salt

Peel and thinly slice the red onions, either by hand or using a mandolin.

Mix the remaining ingredients in a saucepan, dissolving the sugar, and bring to a boil.

Cool down, then pour over the onions. Refrigerate, will be ready in 24 hours.

Makes 1 quart

caper aioli

1½ cups Kewpie mayo
¼ cup chopped capers
1 teaspoon lemon pepper
1 lemon, zested and juiced
½ teaspoon sugar
½ teaspoon pickle juice

Blend all ingredients and let sit for at least an hour to meld flavors.

dinner specialties...

What's For Supper?!

We invite you to join us for supper Wednesday thru Saturday nights while we prepare a delightful dinner entree. Eat with us or take home and enjoy in your own home!

Wednesday Night is Jesse's evening to create a vegetarian delight. Her meals will please the vegetarian and the meat eaters!

The remaining nights, you will find Laurel in the kitchen with a glass of wine in one hand and a whisk in the other! The use of the best of seasonal produce, meats or seafood, a splash of wine and culinary imagination, ensures you of a memorable dining experience.

With the success of our event nights and the opening of the patio, it was time to expand our hours to stay open until 9 p.m. With this decision, Doug left his job at Theo's to join our team full-time. We continued to serve the daily chalkboard menu, but now we would offer a dinner special. With a small kitchen—basically just a gas range, prep table, and sinks—our creativity and efficiency were tested. It did not, however, stop us from putting out delicious meals. It was at this time that my grilled lemon chicken dish was conceived.

grilled lemon chicken

1 lemon
2 tablespoons olive oil
2 chicken breasts
lemon pepper
thyme leaves
fennel seed
1 yellow onion, sliced
1 red pepper, sliced
2 tablespoons minced garlic
12 canned artichoke hearts quarters
1 cup chardonnay, non-oaked
2 tablespoons butter
2 handfuls spinach
½ cup feta crumbles
1 tablespoon crushed pink peppercorns

Cut the lemon in half and grill facedown until lightly charred and caramelized.

Heat the olive oil in a large sauté pan. Dredge the chicken breasts with lemon pepper, thyme, and fennel seed, pressing it into the meat. Place in a hot pan, cook until golden brown, then turn over. Add the lemon, facedown, then add the onion, peppers, and artichokes. Rub the garlic on top of the chicken. Continue to cook, stirring the vegetables often.

When chicken is almost cooked through, slowly pour in the wine, and butter, and let the alcohol steam off. Fold in the spinach, heating until just wilted. Remove the chicken breasts from the pan. Pour the remaining pan contents onto serving plates, including the juices. Lay the chicken breasts over the top, lightly squeeze the juices from the grilled lemon over the vegetables and place back on the plate. Finish with feta. Garnish with crumbled peppercorns.

Serves 2

in-store shopping...

With all the wonderful ingredients we had in the deli and gourmet shop it was fun to peruse the stock, basket in hand, selecting "chopped style" what would become the evening's supper. With each special, we would usually cook with and pair the dish with the perfect wine.

peachy spinach and bacon salad with blue cheese dressing

1 pound thick-sliced bacon
¼ cup brown sugar
1 teaspoon red pepper flakes
2 white onions, cut in 1-inch-thick slices, then cut in quarters
salt and pepper
2 tablespoons butter
4 peaches, cut into ½-inch wedges
1/4 cup riesling wine
1 cup pecans
1 tablespoon maple syrup
½ pound spinach
1/2 cup Doug's blue cheese dressing

Line a baking sheet with parchment paper, lay the bacon slices in a single layer, and sprinkle with the brown sugar and pepper flakes. Bake at 350 degrees for approximately 20 minutes. Let cool, then cut into large pieces.

Sauté the onions in olive oil until lightly browned. Season with salt and pepper.

Melt the butter in the sauté pan, add the peaches, toss until warmed, then on high heat slowly add the Riesling, let reduce, and add the pecans and maple syrup. Do not overcook the peaches!

In a large bowl, toss all the ingredients together with the spinach. Drizzle lightly with blue cheese dressing, serve immediately.

Serves 8

doug's blue cheese dressing

18 ounces Kewpie mayo
½ pound buttermilk blue cheese, crumbled
1 tablespoon worcestershire sauce
2 teaspoon garlic salt
¼ cup buttermilk

Combine all ingredients and mix well.

Makes 1 pint

Hint: Buttermilk blue cheese is a creamy Wisconsin cheese made from fresh raw milk. It has a mild, yet tangy flavor, aged for at least two months.

time to move...

As each year passed, we were slowly outgrowing the space. Even with the building's structural issues mounting, I knew that it would take a lot to convince Doug to relocate the business again. Well . . . news hit that the current tenant of the old Sioux Falls Brewing Company space was closing. The north end of downtown was being redistricted into Uptown. New condos and retail areas were going to be built. I yearned to get back to the first building I fell in love with. Needless to say, shortly thereafter, our friends gathered again to help me move to the place I had genuinely thought would be home forever.

Chapter Seven

taking on a bigger project

food n' fermentations III...

As in all my places, I never hired designers; creating the ambiance myself was as exciting as developing the menu. I was inspired by the work of local artist Chad Garnes, of Blue Devil Creative. His unique designs with metal would tie in perfectly with the "warehouse chic" atmosphere I was trying to produce.

Starting with the tired old wooden bar, he covered the top with stainless steel that we had all taken hammers to for a distressed look. It was finished with riveted copper metal strips as trim. Layers of polyurethane were meticulously applied to not only seal the surface but give it a lustrous glow that reflected the red color of wine. A sheet-metal wrap completed the look.

Chad also designed nontraditional racking for the wine. Unique angles and unexpected curves displayed the bottles like no other. The refabricated heavy steel against the stone wall was stunning. For another surprise display, he painted and repurposed the back end of an old De Soto car.

His talents were then channeled into painting murals. Exposed brick and stucco, along with grapevines, were reproduced onto the one area that was drywalled. With an air brush in hand, he honored winemakers that had been so gracious to us on trips to Napa, by painting their winery logos or labels from the bottles. Scott Harvey, from Scott Harvey Wines, was one of these people. He was not only a fabulous host at his home, but he visited Sioux Falls often, building a fan base at our wine events. He even gifted Chad with an autographed magnum of his InZINerator wine for his work.

With tables and chairs, originally from the Sioux Falls Brewing Company, in place, there was an added layer of comfort. Historic photos of downtown and South Dakota breweries graced the walls. The wicker chianti bottles, collected from the preparation of many pots of our tomato soup, hung from the massive beams. This would be a room where many great memories would be made.

From the tasting bar, you could look through the huge glass panels that had once enclosed the brewery but now surrounded my cheese and charcuterie cave. We covered the walls with chalkboard paint, where we listed many of the cheeses we carried. The varieties more than doubled what we'd had at the previous shop.

All of the FnF team acquired a love for fromage, but Eli DeGroff became a true turophile. We jokingly called him the Cheese Whiz. He exercised his palate to find the perfect wine pairing.

I loved nurturing his passion, so together we started a club named Friends of Fromage. Once a month, we presented three different cheeses, served with the proper accompaniments and wines. The comparison tastings certainly brought about tantalizing conversation.

The cheese cave was in the center of the room, dividing the wine shop and bistro from the gourmet shop. You walked through a grain bin to begin your shopping. Appropriately, it was filled with whiskey, vodka, and gins! There were scattered tables positioned by the large windows for diners that wanted to take in the sunshine streaming in from Phillips Avenue. Many times, those tables were filled by friends enjoying lunch, a glass of wine, and shopping, all in one location.

big hits...

Shopping lunches were popular. I could hear the ladies laughing while I was back in the kitchen cooking. Many would pop in through the door that opened from the cheese cave, to say hello and hopefully get a taste of what I was working on. This helped to motivate my creativity.

We offered many of the sandwiches we'd had at the previous location, but with some new twists. Our featured turkey sandwich was one of them. It can be a little nerve-racking to make changes to something that is already a big seller, but this was worth the risk. By switching out the port salut cheese for a chèvre orange marmalade mix and adding wine to the cranberries, magic was made. Suddenly this sandwich was our biggest seller, and it continued to be until the day I retired.

turkey cranberry sandwich

8 slices cranberry wild rice bread
2 tablespoons butter, softened
4 ounces chèvre cheese
4 tablespoons orange marmalade
1 (4-ounce) bag spinach
1 pound sliced turkey breast
1 cup whole cranberry sauce (you can buy it canned, but we made our own)

Brush one side of each slice of bread with butter and grill until lightly browned.

Mix the chèvre and orange marmalade together and spread a layer on 4 slices of the bread.

Put down a layer of spinach, then turkey. Spoon a thick layer of cranberry sauce on top.

Top with the other slices of bread.

Makes 4

Chèvre

Chèvre is a creamy, tangy goat cheese that promotes development of good intestinal bacteria and is low in lactose, making it a healthier choice from the world of fromage.

cranberry sauce

¾ cup sugar
¾ cup merlot wine
12 ounces fresh cranberries
¼ cup honey
¼ teaspoon ground clove
zest and juice of 1 orange
½ cup pecan pieces

In a saucepan, dissolve the sugar and red wine together. Add the cranberries, honey, clove, and orange. Bring to a slow boil and simmer until thickened, stirring frequently. Let cool, fold in pecan pieces, then refrigerate.

With a cave full of cheese and charcuterie our focaccia torte was a showcase of Italian delights. The bread was baked in a round cake pan for a tall, unique presentation. When the wedge is warmed, it becomes spongy, perfect for dipping into a cup of chianti tomato basil soup (see page 71).

italian focaccia torte

2 packets dry active yeast
1 tablespoon honey
1 cup warm water
½ cup semolina flour
2½ cups flour
½ tablespoon salt
1 tablespoon fresh minced rosemary
2 tablespoons olive oil
1 tablespoon butter
1 teaspoon italian seasoning

Filling

1/2 cup basil pesto
¼ pound genoa salami, sliced
¼ pound capicola ham, sliced
2 tomatoes, thin sliced
1 small white onion, thin sliced
2 roasted red peppers, spread open
1 cup black olives, sliced
¼ pound provolone cheese, sliced

Make the focaccia: Mix the yeast and honey in the warm water, stirring to dissolve the honey, then allow to sit until bubbly, about 10 minutes. Combine the flours, salt, rosemary, and olive oil in a mixer bowl and add the yeast mixture. Mix with a dough hook, adding additional flour if it's too sticky to handle.

Coat a bowl with butter and place the dough in the bowl, cover with a towel, and let rise in a warm place until it's doubled in size, about an hour.

On a floured surface, punch down the dough and lightly knead for about a minute.

Lightly oil two 8-inch round pans, divide the dough in half, press each portion into one of the pans, cover, and let rise for another half hour.

Press fingertips into dough to create indentations, then brush the top with olive oil and dust with Italian seasoning.

Bake at 400 degrees until golden brown, about 20 minutes.

Assemble the torte: Slice the focaccia round in half horizontally. Spread a thick layer of pesto on the bottom half.

Continue layering each of the other ingredients on top of the focaccia, then gently press the two halves together.

Cut into 6 wedges, tightly wrap each piece in Saran wrap, and refrigerate for 1 hour.

When you are ready to serve, warm them while still wrapped in the microwave for a soft and spongy texture or unwrap them and warm them in the oven for a crispier sandwich.

Serves 6

On one of the symphony evenings, we were honored to have Midori, a world-renown concert violinist, stop in for a short presentation for supporters. She has played most of her life, having been invited to perform with the New York Philharmonic Orchestra when she was only eleven years old. Midori was recently chosen as a recipient of one of the 43rd Kennedy Center Honors for her lifetime achievement in the arts.

While the women were shopping, the guys often enjoyed a bowl of our hunter's stew, some crusty bread, and a glass of hearty red wine. Through the years its popularity grew. We were always a supporter of our South Dakota Symphony Orchestra. In return, we were supported by concertgoers who would enjoy a bite to eat with us before the performance. On those evenings, one of the most requested menu items was this dish.

hunter's stew

12 fingerling potatoes
olive oil
himalayan pink sea salt
2 tablespoons olive oil
1 (4-ounce) rabbit sausage
1 (4-ounce) pheasant sausage
1 (4-ounce) venison sausages
1 large yellow onion, quartered
1 ½ cup demi-glace
1 tablespoon cracked black pepper
2 teaspoons dried thyme
1 teaspoon rubbed sage
2 handfuls spinach
2 tablespoons shaved parmigiano reggiano
1 teaspoon crushed pink peppercorns

Cut the fingerling potatoes in half lengthwise and rub with olive oil. Put them on a baking tray and sprinkle with pink sea salt crystals. Bake in a 350-degree oven for 25 minutes. While baking, cut the sausages in four pieces and quarter the onions.

Make demi-glace as instructed on the package. (You can make your own at home, but it is a long process. If you have the patience, it is worth the effort. I personally am a fan of Robert Irvine's.) Once the demi-glace has thickened, add the pepper and herbs.

In a large sauté pan, heat the olive oil on medium heat, add the sausage chunks, and brown on all sides. Add the onions, lightly brown, and then add the cooked potatoes. When the sausage is cooked through, pour in the herbed demi-glace. Stir well and let simmer for 5 minutes.

When ready to serve, fold in the spinach and continue to cook until just wilted.

Pour into serving bowls, garnish with cheese and pink peppercorns, and serve with bread to get the last drippings!

Serves 2

women empowerment...

For the first couple of years in this location, life was exciting. I was writing wine articles for etc. for her magazine and was featured in many other publications, such as this one in City Style. We were hosting dinners with some of the finest winemakers and started a group for women interested in learning about wine.

It started out with a casual gathering of about six ladies. We selected wine and cheese, then shared our knowledge with each other. Perry Groten, from KELO-TV, did a great piece about our group and the empowerment of women in the wine industry. During this interview he called us the GrapeGals, which became the name that carried on for the next thirteen years.

Suddenly, our group grew in popularity, and we were now forty strong. Each lady would purchase a bottle, then stand up and tell everyone why she bought it. From pretty labels to great memories, the reasons varied. We moved from table to table sampling each other's wine. Not only was this an educational gathering, it was also a social event. New friendships were formed as we continued to meet on a monthly basis.

I have found that many of my close relationships are born through a shared passion for wine and food. One great example would be Diana D'Hanis, Mike's sister from Beloit, Wisconsin. Her culinary beginnings paralleled my own, learning to cook with her Grandma, then graduating to help with Friday fish fries. Fortunate to have a cousin Todd who was a chef, she became his sidekick at the Liberty Inn in Beloit, then moved on to private catering gigs.

When she was in town, we would end up cooking something together. We laughed through an entire day making mozzarella and ricotta. Every time I eat a caprese salad and bite into the cheese, I chuckle to myself remembering what fun we shared. Set up in a garage, we proudly helped prepare the family dinner for her nephew Kenny and his fiancée Amanda's wedding. But one of the best things Diana cooked, in my opinion, was her Grandma Frances's strudel.

Mike would receive a holiday box from her that always had the strudel in it. It was some of the best I'd ever tasted, so of course, I wanted to share it with others. I thought it would be great to have her do a demonstration on a Saturday afternoon.

The butcher block table was set up in the bistro area with all the ingredients she would need. I'm not quite sure that Mike conveyed to Diana that she would be doing this for the public, but being a trouper, she willingly went through the process. Everyone loved it, and after a couple brewskis, I believe she forgave Mike.

Diana has since passed away, but our memories and her recipe for this strudel will always continue to live on.

APPLE STRUDEL

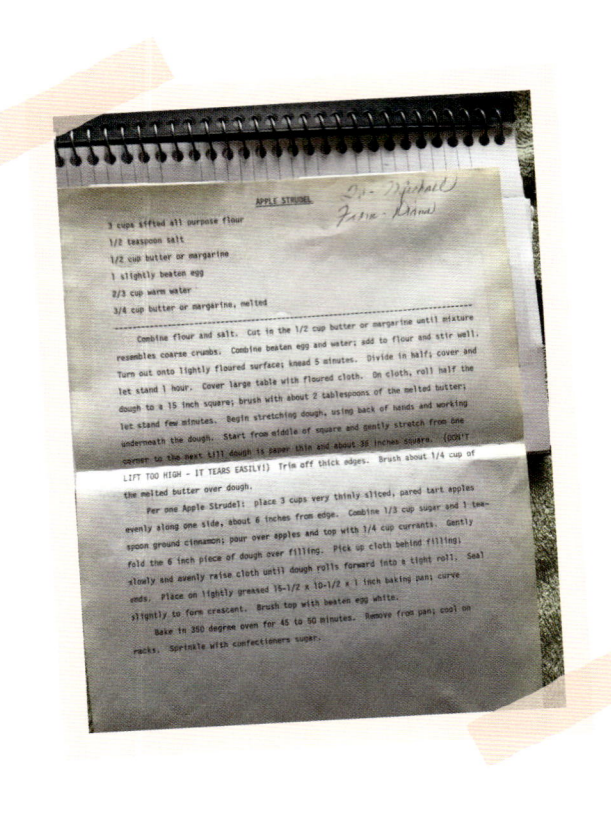

Dr. Michael
From - Anna

3 cups sifted all purpose flour
1/2 teaspoon salt
1/2 cup butter or margarine
1 slightly beaten egg
2/3 cup warm water
3/4 cup butter or margarine, melted

Combine flour and salt. Cut in the 1/2 cup butter or margarine until mixture resembles coarse crumbs. Combine beaten egg and water; add to flour and stir well. Turn out onto lightly floured surface; knead 5 minutes. Divide in half; cover and let stand 1 hour. Cover large table with floured cloth. On cloth, roll half the dough to a 15 inch square; brush with about 2 tablespoons of the melted butter; let stand few minutes. Begin stretching dough, using back of hands and working underneath the dough. Start from middle of square and gently stretch from one corner to the next. LIFT dough is paper thin and about 36 inches square. (DON'T LIFT TOO HIGH - IT TEARS EASILY!) Trim off thick edges. Brush about 1/4 cup of the melted butter over dough.

Per one Apple Strudel: place 3 cups very thinly sliced, pared tart apples evenly along one side, about 6 inches from edge. Combine 1/3 cup sugar and 1 teaspoon ground cinnamon; pour over apples and top with 1/4 cup currants. Gently fold the 6 inch piece of dough over filling. Pick up cloth behind filling; slowly and evenly raise cloth until dough rolls forward into a tight roll. Seal ends. Place on lightly greased 15-1/2 x 10-1/2 x 1 inch baking pan; curve slightly to form crescent. Brush top with beaten egg white.

Bake in 350 degree oven for 45 to 50 minutes. Remove from pan; cool on racks. Sprinkle with confectioners sugar.

economic crisis of 2008...

It appeared that we had a huge success. We anxiously awaited the groundbreaking of the Uptown project that would bring more retail and housing to our north end neighborhood. Then the financial crisis of 2008 hit, the worst economic disaster since the Great Depression of 1929. Construction came to a grinding halt, projects were postponed. Day by day, business began to slow down. Our specialty products were a luxury, not a necessity. We tried to hold on for as long as we could, but eventually my dreams shattered. Standing in front of all our employees and telling them that we would be closing was one of the hardest things I ever had to do.

Chapter Eight

back on my feet

the market on phillips...

When you fall down, you brush off your knees and start running again. I believed that moving back to the heart of downtown and scaling back on the square footage, we could rebuild and be a success again. With the financial hit we took, we would need partners to begin this new venture. Blessed to have friends that believed in us, within three months, Doug and I would be meeting with Terry and Lynette Kelley, James Jacobson, and Albert Brooks to start our new venture, The Market on Phillips.

It was like a barn raising; friends and past customers all rallied to help. Swift Contractors built the large tasting bar and counter, plus tore out the display windows to allow for an outdoor patio. Eli created signage and our friend, Bobby T, stopped in to help Doug and Terry with the long, arduous task of putting together all the wine racks. Local artist, Chad Lubbers, painted our logos. There were so many others that lent a hand to help us finally open our doors, we were thankful to them all.

The shelves were filled with the finest of gourmet groceries, rivaling what we had at Food n' Fermentations. With so many great items to choose from, it was easy to be creative when making gift baskets and catered cheese boards. Our reputation for quality helped build this part of the business to new highs.

To increase those sales, I started writing a wine blog for the Argus Leader and articles for Now!Pavilion. We were also featured in many articles by others. One of my favorite pictures of The Market partners was taken for the annual publication of the Talk of the Town.

Along with the retail wine and grocery area, this location was set up specifically for wine and cheese tastings. The large bar had a television to allow for Skype classes and direct visits with the winemakers. We had two large tables and ample bar seating to accommodate about thirty guests.

five for $5 WINE TASTING

Doug was a schoolteacher before getting into the hospitality industry. He wanted to utilize those skills, which led to the beginning of our Five for $5 program. This was a daily tasting of five different wines for $5. If you purchased a bottle of one of the wines he was sampling, your tasting was free. This was extremely successful, becoming a trademark of the business, wine shopping at its finest.

Twice a year, Doug also held a huge Crazy Day Sale. Cases of wine would be sold at amazingly low prices. The evening before, our longtime customers were invited for a sneak peek advantage. While he was sampling the wine, I served little tidbits of cheese and charcuterie. It quickly turned into a social night out and our biggest day of sales.

our exclusive clubs...

The GrapeGals had their triumphant return here at the market. We changed the format from freestyle to a "structured" program. I use structured loosely as it could be a challenge at times to get all the ladies' attention, especially after the first couple of wines. But Elaine Elias and Ashley Waddell, our wine reps with Cask & Cork Distributing, presented their wines with patience and grace.

Each month they selected a different country or wine region to feature. I enjoyed preparing foods indigenous to the area to pair with them. We made a passport book that the ladies could store their tasting notes in. Each time they attended an event they received a stamp. Most of them had full books by the end of the year!

The GrapeGal logo was unknowingly designed by local artist Kiel Mutschelknaus. Our partner James had attended a fundraiser and purchased a painting by Kiel. When he brought it down to hang in The Market on Phillips, I fell in love with it immediately. The artist's mother, Jane, happened to be a GrapeGal, so I asked her if Kiel would give us permission to use his art as the logo. He agreed, so the ladies now had an official emblem.

There was something incredibly special about this group. It wasn't just about the wine and food. This was an opportunity for the women to gather, celebrate their friendships, and be sympathetic when one of us was down. That last one was never more evident than when Elaine started her battle with cancer. Let's just say she had a large support group.

Elaine was also a great cook, so we loved sharing recipes and swapping Tupperware bowls of culinary treats. I prepared a lot of dishes for the GrapeGals, but there was one that meant the most to me. In Elaine's honor I used her recipe for lasagna and poured her favorite Italian wines. That night all the ladies got to share a taste of her passion and take home a copy of the recipe.

ELAINE'S Quick Spaghetti Sauce

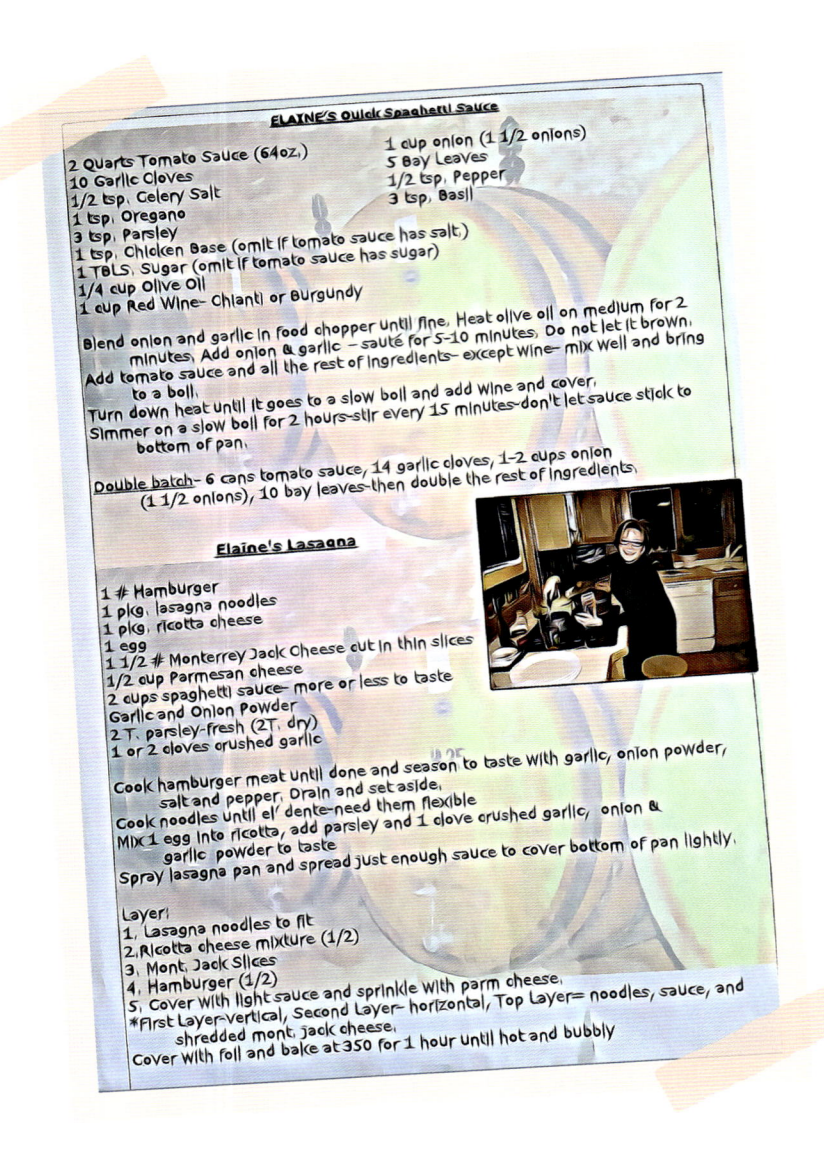

2 Quarts Tomato Sauce (64oz.)
10 Garlic Cloves
1/2 tsp. Celery Salt
1 tsp. Oregano
3 tsp. Parsley
1 tsp. Chicken Base (omit if tomato sauce has salt.)
1 TBLS. Sugar (omit if tomato sauce has sugar)
1/4 cup Olive Oil
1 cup Red Wine- Chianti or Burgundy
1 cup onion (1 1/2 onions)
5 Bay Leaves
1/2 tsp. Pepper
3 tsp. Basil

Blend onion and garlic in food chopper until fine. Heat olive oil on medium for 2 minutes. Add onion & garlic – sauté for 5-10 minutes. Do not let it brown. Add tomato sauce and all the rest of ingredients- except wine- mix well and bring to a boil.
Turn down heat until it goes to a slow boil and add wine and cover.
Simmer on a slow boil for 2 hours-stir every 15 minutes-don't let sauce stick to bottom of pan.

Double batch- 6 cans tomato sauce, 14 garlic cloves, 1-2 cups onion (1 1/2 onions), 10 bay leaves-then double the rest of ingredients.

Elaine's Lasagna

1 # Hamburger
1 pkg. lasagna noodles
1 pkg. ricotta cheese
1 egg
1 1/2 # Monterrey Jack Cheese cut in thin slices
1/2 cup Parmesan cheese
2 cups spaghetti sauce- more or less to taste
Garlic and Onion Powder
2 T. parsley-fresh (2T. dry)
1 or 2 cloves crushed garlic

Cook hamburger meat until done and season to taste with garlic, onion powder, salt and pepper. Drain and set aside.
Cook noodles until el' dente-need them flexible
Mix 1 egg into ricotta, add parsley and 1 clove crushed garlic, onion & garlic powder to taste
Spray lasagna pan and spread just enough sauce to cover bottom of pan lightly.

Layer:
1. Lasagna noodles to fit
2. Ricotta cheese mixture (1/2)
3. Mont. Jack Slices
4. Hamburger (1/2)
5. Cover with light sauce and sprinkle with parm cheese.
*First Layer-vertical, Second Layer- horizontal, Top Layer= noodles, sauce, and shredded mont. jack cheese.
Cover with foil and bake at 350 for 1 hour until hot and bubbly

Anyone who was given a jar of Elaine's green chili was fortunate. It was one of the best—okay, the best I have ever had. Before she passed away, she finally shared her recipe with me. Every time I make this sauce, I swear that she is in the room with me. I believe she would want me to share it with you.

elaine's green chili sauce

3 pounds top loin boneless pork loin
2 quarts water
¼ cup olive oil
5 large garlic cloves, minced
1 cup flour
4 pounds canned chopped green chilis
1 (16-ounce) can peeled tomatoes, chopped fine
1 teaspoon cumin
2 teaspoon onion powder
1 tablespoon chicken broth paste
1 (7.75-ounce) can El Pato salsa de jalapeño

Trim excess fat from the pork, dice in small pieces, brown in a stockpot, and once crispy, add 1 quart of the water, bring to a low boil, and continue to cook for 1 hour.

Save the fatty water and cut the pork in small pieces. In another stockpot, brown it with olive oil and garlic. Add flour to coat meat. Add the chilis, tomatoes, and the other quart of water.

To the pot with fatty water, add the spices, paste and salsa.

Continue to boil both pots for another hour, stirring occasionally.

Combine both pots and simmer until thickened, 1–2 hours.

Makes approximately 3 quarts

New Chili

In the late 1800s, Fabian Garcia, one of five members of the first graduating class of New Mexico's College of Agriculture, developed the new long green chili pepper that is used in this recipe.

The guys were feeling left out and wanted their own evening to gather, thus the Wine Club for Men was established. This group definitely had no structure. Having a penchant for fine wines, they either brought special bottles from their own home cellar or bought from our stellar section. I would prepare food that could be held in Crock-Pots or displayed on trays. They ate and drank at will throughout the night.

Quite often they would bring me wild game from their hunting expeditions. From pheasant to elk, I enjoyed the challenge. Thank you, Jack Miller, for all your tasty contributions!

pulled elk roast

1 (4-pound) elk roast
flour
salt and pepper
4 dried chipotles, crushed
rubbed sage
½ pound bacon, chopped
2 cup beef stock
2 cup beaujolais nouveau wine
2 yellow onions, quartered
rosemary sprigs
8 cloves garlic

Rub the roast liberally with flour, salt, pepper, chipotle, and sage, pressing it into the meat.

In a large, deep skillet cook the bacon until crispy. Remove and save for later, then brown the roast in the bacon fat for 5 minutes on each side. Remove meat and place in a roasting pan.

In the skillet, sprinkle 2 tablespoons of flour and slowly add the beef stock, stirring to release the brown bits and start to thicken.

Pour this alongside the meat in a roasting pan. Add the wine.

Line the side with onions and top with rosemary and garlic.

Put on a tight lid or wrap snugly with aluminum foil and bake at 275 degrees until tender and pulls apart, about 5 hours.

Pull apart the meat and top with saved bacon bits.

You're ready to grab a bun and enjoy!

Yields approximately 2 pounds of cooked meat

Beaujolais Nouveau

Beaujolais Nouveau is made from the gamay grape grown in the Beaujolais region of France. It is a celebrated young wine that is bottled as soon as fermentation has taken place and released for sale on the third Thursday of November.

pheasant with morel mushrooms

1 (3-pound) pheasant
salt and pepper
2 tablespoons thyme
1 cup chardonnay
¼ cup olive oil
flour
1 yellow onion, cut in half then thinly sliced
2 cups chicken stock
8–10 ounces fresh morel mushrooms, cleaned
4 tablespoons butter

Sprinkle the pheasant with salt, pepper, and 1 tablespoon thyme, cover with ½ cup of the wine and the olive oil, and marinate for at least 2 hours.

Remove the meat from the marinade. Save the marinade for later.

Roll the pheasant in flour, and in a Dutch oven brown lightly on both sides for a few minutes. Remove the meat from the pan temporarily.

In the same Dutch oven, pour in the marinade, stirring to deglaze the pan. Add the onions. Cook until the onions are translucent.

Pour in the remaining wine and the stock, and bring to a boil.

Place the pheasant back in the pot, cover, and lower heat to simmer until the pheasant is tender. This may take 1 to 2 hours.

When ready to serve, lightly sauté the mushrooms in the butter, sprinkle with salt, pepper, and the remaining thyme. Add to the pheasant.

Serve over rice.

Serves 4

The time to Forage

The foragers say that when the leaves of the oak tree are the size of a mouse's ear, and my Gramma said it was when the lilacs bloom, but either way, at that time there is only a three-week period where you can find the elusive spring morel mushroom.

confit of pheasant rillettes

2 whole wild pheasants, quartered
salt and pepper to taste
1 teaspoon nutmeg
1 teaspoon rubbed sage
2 teaspoons dried thyme
2 pounds duck fat
6 bay leaves
fresh sage leaves and lingonberries for garnish

Season the pheasants with salt, pepper, nutmeg, rubbed sage, and dried thyme.

In a dutch oven, melt 2 tablespoons of the duck fat and brown the pheasant on both sides.

Add the remaining duck fat, and if it doesn't cover the meat, top it off with olive oil. Put in the bay leaves.

Cover tightly and bake at 250 degrees until the meat falls off the bones, 4–6 hours.

Remove the meat from the pan, saving the fat.

Remove the skin, place in a blender with ¼ cup of the reserved fat, and blend until smooth.

Debone the pheasant and shred the meat.

Place the meat and blended skin in a mixer fit with paddle and whip until desired texture. I like it a little chunky. Season to taste.

Press into ramekins and garnish with sage leaves and lingonberries. Spoon enough of the reserved fat to just cover the sage leaves.

Cover with Saran wrap and refrigerate to firm up.

Take out of the refrigerator 15 minutes before serving with bread and lingonberry jam.

Makes 6 – 8 ramekins

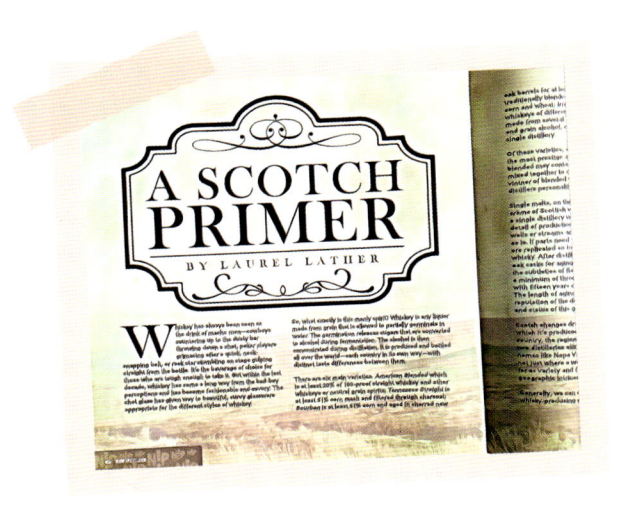

Our education didn't stop with wine. Whiskey sales were skyrocketing and the number of craft distilleries had more than quintupled. Our inventory of single-malt scotch and bourbons was growing weekly. I even wrote a piece about them in the Now!Pavilion magazine.

Legally, we could not serve cocktails, but we could sample if the distillery rep was present. So we started the Whiskey Society. Franny Gergen helped with organizing the speakers and hosting presentations. The food that I served was either paired with the whiskey or was made with it. We had a loyal following that was very inquisitive. The classroom tastings were exciting, but they really loved when things were hands-on. I believe the most popular gathering was when we blended our own special aged cocktail.

Here are a few of their favorite recipes . . .

bangers and colcannon with irish whiskey glaze

2 pounds yukon gold potatoes, quartered
¼ pound bacon, minced
¼ small head cabbage, small diced
½ tablespoon dill seed
10 tablespoons butter
salt and pepper
½ cup heavy cream
milk (if needed)
¼ cup olive oil
4 irish or english banger links, cut in thirds
1 large onion, thick sliced
1 teaspoon minced garlic
6 ounces sun-dried tomatoes
4 ounces sliced mushrooms
2 tablespoons dijon mustard
2 tablespoons worcestershire sauce
3 tablespoons flour
1 cup irish whiskey

Colcannon: Cook the potatoes until fork tender, then drain.

Meanwhile, cook the bacon until almost crispy, add the cabbage, dill seed, and 2 tablespoons of the butter, season with salt and pepper, and cook until tender.

Mash the potatoes, add the cabbage mixture, 6 more tablespoons of the butter, and the cream . . . add milk if needed to get to a smoother consistency.

Bangers: Heat the oil in a large sauté pan, cook the sausages until just golden brown, take them out, and set aside for later.

Add the onions to the same pan and sauté until translucent. Add the garlic, the remaining 2 tablespoons butter, the sun dried tomatoes, mushrooms, mustard, and worcestershire. Sprinkle in the flour and let it cook for a few minutes.

Blend in the whiskey and simmer for 10 minutes. Add the sausage and continue to simmer to reduce by half, about 10 minutes.

Divide the colcannon mash between 4 plates, top with sausage onion mixture.

Garnish with clover.

Serves 4

whiskey braised onion and cheese soup

1 cup plus 2 tablespoons butter
2 carrots, shredded
4 stalks celery, finely chopped
½ cup flour
8 cups chicken stock
2 cups heavy cream
1 pound cheddar, shredded
½ pound smoked gouda, shredded
½ teaspoon nutmeg
1 teaspoon black pepper
1 tablespoon stone ground mustard
1 teaspoon worcestershire sauce
2 yellow onions, sliced
1 tablespoon honey
¾ cup whiskey

Melt 1 cup of the butter in a large sauce pot, add the carrots and celery, and sauté until tender.

Sprinkle with flour, cook for 5 minutes, then slowly add the stock, bring to a boil, reduce heat, and simmer for about a half hour.

With an immersion blender, puree the vegetable mixture.

Add the cream, cheese, nutmeg, pepper, mustard, and worcestershire, and stir until the cheese is melted.

Meanwhile, melt the remaining 2 tablespoons butter in a sauté pan, add the onions and honey, stir while caramelizing to a light brown color, add the whiskey, and reduce.

Fold the onions into the soup.

Can be served as a soup or cooked down for spreadable bread dip.

Serves 6 - 8

cold brew irish whiskey glazed corned beef with cheddar mashers and napa cabbage

5–6 pounds corned beef brisket
6 stalks celery
½–¾ cup stone ground mustard
½ cup pickling spice
12 bay leaves
2 cups Jameson Cold Brew Irish Whiskey
1 (12-ounce) can stout beer
2 cups strong brewed coffee

Brisket Preparation: Trim excess fat from the brisket, leaving a thin layer. Lightly rinse the meat with cool running water to wash off the salty brine it was packaged in. Lay the celery stalks in the bottom of a roasting pan, using them as a raft to keep the meat off the surface. Place the meat, fat side up, on the celery. Spread the mustard evenly onto the meat and finish with a layer of the spices. Pour the whiskey, beer, and coffee in the pan, off to the side, avoiding the spice cap. Add water, if necessary, to bring liquids up to one third of the pan. Cover tightly with foil and bake in a 325-degree oven until it pulls apart easily, 3–4 hours. Let it rest for half an hour before slicing.

Glaze Preparation: Pour the pan juices into a large saucepan and bring to a boil. Turn heat down and allow the glaze to simmer until it has reduced to 2 cups, or until it thoroughly coats the back of the spoon.

Serves 8 - 10

cheddar mashers

3 pounds yukon gold potatoes, cut in quarters
1/2 cup grated irish cheddar
5 tablespoons irish butter
2 egg yolk
2/3 cup heavy cream
1 1/2 teaspoon sea salt
1/2 teaspoon white pepper

Boil the potatoes in salted water until tender, then drain well. Put back in the pot and add the cheddar and butter. Mash or whip together until the cheese is melted. Whisk the egg yolk into the cream, then add to the potatoes along with salt and pepper. Mash until creamy.

Serves 8 - 10

Napa Cabbage: Thinly slice 1 large head of cabbage, melt 1 tablespoon irish butter in a sauté pan, add the cabbage, and cook only until wilted.

Serves 8 - 10

thinking of whiskey always brings this story to mind...

After a night of celebrating my birthday, we were awoken in the wee hours of the morning by a phone call from the police department. We were told to meet them at the store. Rushing down in just our jammies, we were greeted by multiple squad cars, lights flashing. They escorted us into the shop, explaining that there had been a robbery where entry had been gained through our back door.

A section of the large, very heavy shelving units had been pulled away from the wall. Décor items and the products that had been on the shelves were scattered about on the floor. A hole had been cut through the wall into the neighboring jewelry shop. The robbers had crawled through, staying on the floor to avoid the jeweler's alarm. Three jewelry cases had been emptied. It was definitely a professional job. They had to have scoped out both stores to find the perfect spot to cut the hole. It was a surreal site.

As we inspected our store for any theft, we found that a bar stool had been moved next to the cheese cooler. On the floor next to it was a partially drunk bottle of Crown Royal whiskey and an empty wrapper from a chunk of smoked gouda cheese. Apparently, one of the robbers had had the time for a late-night snack . . .

cooking dinners...

Our original game plan was to only serve cheese and charcuterie plates at the tasting bar; there would be no dinners. The only exceptions would be for the GrapeGals and the Whiskey Society. Then we started holding Skype tastings with wine legends such as Randall Grahm from Bonny Doon Winery. We snuck in a "Lunch with a Winemaker," featuring Jeff Mathy from Vellum Wine Craft. Before I knew it, we were hosting various wine dinners and private small parties.

One of our "exceptions" was a dinner for Sally Jefferson from the Wine Institute. She was in town to give advice to a group of individuals trying to make changes to the South Dakota wine shipping laws. For this event I prepared one of my favorite hearty salads, spring duck and blackberry.

spring duck and blackberry salad

12 fiddlehead fern fronds
2 duck breasts, skin-on, seasoned with salt and pepper
2 sprigs of fresh rosemary
12 morel mushrooms, cut in half and cleaned
4 green onions, cut in 2-inch pieces
18 blackberries
6 strawberries, cut in half
1 bunch arugula
2 tablespoons balsamic glaze
½ teaspoon ground ginger
½ teaspoon minced garlic
1 tablespoon grated sap sago cheese
1 tablespoon pinot noir wine
4 tablespoons olive oil

Boil the fiddleheads in salted water for 15 minutes and drain on paper towels.

Place the duck breasts skin-side-down in a hot pan, cook about 15 minutes, turn over, dip rosemary in the duck fat then lay it on top of the duck skin, and cook for another 5 minutes, should be mid-rare. Take the breasts and rosemary out of the pan, remove the skin, and set the breasts aside.

Cut the skin into small pieces. Add back to the duck fat and cook until crispy, then drain on paper towels.

Add the morels, fiddleheads, and green onion pieces to the duck fat, sauté for just a few minutes to brown, then drain on paper towels.

Mix the balsamic glaze, ginger, garlic, cheese, wine, and olive oil. Lightly toss with arugula and berries, divide salad between two serving plates. Top with morels, onion, and ferns.

Thinly slice duck breast, layover salad.

Serves 2

Sap Sago

Sap Sago is a hard grating cheese originally produced by monks in Glarus, Switzerland. It is made from skim milk and blue fenugreek clover. The clover gives it the signature lime-green color and funky herbaceous flavor.

big bertha the grill...

What a lot of people didn't realize was that I was cooking all the food for the events in a backroom makeshift kitchen. Most of it was prepared using Crock-Pots, electric fry pans, and a rotisserie. Occasionally, Doug would bring his Weber grill or Mike would park "Bertha" in the back to help with the larger groups.

Bertha had a celebrated history. Back in 1988, Mike had acquired her for the Northlander, another popular restaurant in Sioux Falls that he was a partner in. She was painted as bright as a fire engine, the belle of the BBQ. As the years passed, the big-barreled grill was a workhorse for many other restaurants, charitable events, and friends' parties. Eventually, the heat and usage began to fade her shiny coat, and Bertha received a new, more practical black paint job.

One of the first things Mike cooked for us on Bertha was goat. Although goat is the most consumed meat in the world, in this country you rarely see it on a menu. It is a healthy choice for dinner, lower in calories, fats, and cholesterol than pork, beef, and chicken. The flavor is mild, with a little lamb earthiness, which makes it very versatile for cooking as it soaks in the flavors of spices and fruit. I made a few different dishes using goat, but the moroccan curry was the most unique.

1 large onion, diced
¼ cup olive oil
1 tablespoon minced garlic
1 tablespoon tomato paste
1 teaspoon red curry paste
1 tablespoon grated ginger root
1 teaspoon ground turmeric
1 teaspoon cumin
1 tablespoon crushed coriander seed
1 cinnamon stick
4 bay leaves
2 tablespoons spicy harissa sauce or 1 teaspoon harissa spice
1 cup vegetable or pork stock
6 dried whole apricots
½ cup raisins
1 tablespoon minced preserved lemon
1 cup mashed potato
1 cup hummus
1 pound cooked goat meat
marcona almonds and green onion for garnish

moroccan goat curry with hummato

Sauté the onions in the olive oil until translucent, then add the garlic and the tomato and red curry pastes, and stir well.

Add the ginger root, all the spices, and the harissa sauce, then slowly stir in the stock.

Add the apricots, raisins, and lemon, and simmer the sauce until thickened, at least a half hour.

Blend the mashed potatoes and hummus together to make hummato, then split between two serving plates.

Place warmed goat meat on the side of the hummato.

Top with curry sauce. Garnish with almonds and green onion.

I served an apricot stuffed with chèvre and mint as an extra treat with the curry.

Serves 2

outgrowing the space...

Once I started cooking again, everyone knew what the consequences would be. After a couple of years of preparing dinners for up to thirty guests out of a closet kitchen, something was going to have to change. If I were to continue cooking, we would need to find a new location that would be more suitable.

I kept my ear to the ground waiting for an opportunity to arise. Months later, it was announced that Tony Keller, owner of the Acoustic restaurant and former short-term chef for us at Food n' Fermentations, was going to close his place. His restaurant was in the Harvester Building. It would offer not only a kitchen, but also more square footage and outdoor seating.

After meeting with Rick Gourley, the owner of the building, I was pretty much convinced that this was the place for me. Many years ago, when Rick was just beginning the renovations to the building, I had walked the floors with him as he explained his vision. At the time I was not ready for such a grandiose project. But now I felt just like Goldilocks, one was too big, one was too small, this one was going to be just right.

Our current partners, happy to have helped get us started, opted out on the move to become a full-blown restaurant again. They decided to turn over ownership to become the most supportive of patrons. To start up a project of this size, however, we would need help. That's when Tom Stritecky became a partner of The Market. Known locally as a big foodie and a pretty darn good cook himself, he had always thought it might be interesting to dabble in the restaurant business. So, along with his wife Becky and friends Brad and Lori Olson, we all would begin a new adventure.

Chapter Nine

my crowning glory

the market...

The Harvester Building had all the charm and history that I adored at Falls Center, so I was excited to now call it home. It was built in 1910 to house offices and warehouse farm equipment for the International Harvester Company. In May of 1917, explosions were heard coming from the building, and shortly afterward the entire second floor was overtaken by flames. The story has it that German spies were riding the rails setting fires to buildings that might be helping the war effort. The arsonists were later caught in Minnesota and confessed to their crimes.

The building's foundation was found to be safe, so she was rebuilt and back in business within a year's time. The Harvester had since then been the home to many residents on the top three floors and various businesses on the main level. We were proud to become one of them.

The saying that it takes a village was never as true as with this project. Doug had an amazing crew that helped him pack and move truckloads of items from the old market. Our friends, Tony and Sue, had a mountain of baskets in the bed of their pickup, hoping they weren't leaving a trail of wicker behind them. Somehow they managed to get everything over without breaking anything, except for our sommelier Franny's toe.

Terry and his crew from Swift Contractors had built such an amazing bar and sturdy shelving for the first market, we had to bring all of it to the new place. The measurements and angles fit perfectly, as if it was all meant to be there. The wine racks filled the walls, the expanse of wood matching the heft of the big wooden beams.

Our new partners showed off their prowess with woodworking. Brad and Lori built a new railing to surround the staircase and a wait station for the patio. Tom repurposed lumber from the building into beautiful dining tables for the lower level.

Local artists came to the rescue for the crowning glory. Steve Bormes, repurposing genius, brought the mood lighting with his art fixtures that were made from olive oil buckets, yogurt churns, potato ricers, and even a teeter-totter from his childhood. Some of the most popular lights were made of pieces from the old Homestake gold mine in Lead, South Dakota.

Molly from the Siouxland Heritage Museums installed life-sized murals featuring the falls and restaurants in downtown Sioux Falls from the early years. Tammy applied a skim-coat burnishing art application to the floors in the lower level.

Months later, with all our friends', partners', past customers', and staff's help and support, we were ready to open the new Market.

With dining out, it is not only the food, but the quality of service and atmosphere that brings guests back. We took pride in customers' comments on how they felt so comfortable at our place. They were met with a smile and, many times, a big hug.

Tables were not crammed in; there was plenty of elbow room. You could shop without feeling you were intruding on someone dining. We even welcomed dogs, bringing them a bowl of water as we greeted the table.

With my promise to Doug that I would never move again, I was determined to make this the best culinary experience in town. If something didn't quite work out or we discovered a more efficient way of doing things, we changed it. Once a year, retail displays were moved and upgrades in furniture occurred. The patio gardens continued to expand.

wine bar cuisine...

We offered a chalkboard menu, so to speak, in the sense that items could change on a daily or monthly basis. We created items inspired by the seasons, showcasing the finest of locally sourced meats and produce accented with unique imported ingredients. Our specialty grocery section was stocked with many of the ingredients used to prepare these dishes.

We called our offerings "Wine Bar Cuisine." Everything, from the sandwiches to the entrées, lent itself to quaffing wine. The portions were hearty enough to share with friends over lively conversation. The "Build your Own Board," featuring artisan cheese and charcuterie, was the perfect example. You would pick from a list of unique, select items, complete with full descriptions. Then our staff would help you purchase the wine that would pair perfectly with your choice. On special nights, I would even take a cart tableside and present my favorites.

I have loved cheese for as long as I can remember. Growing up in Wisconsin certainly helped, but this fondness reaches around the world. As much as I support locals, there is no comparison when it comes to the terroir of fromage. That is why so many cheeses are named after the regions they are made in.

French cheeses happen to be my weakness; that earthy, mushroomy flavor is divine. Its creaminess and pungent aromatics make them addictive. A glass of bubbly or fine burgundy with a crusty baguette takes the experience over the top.

One of the biggest fans of french brie was Leighann. We met at the original Market, coming in to do the "Five for 5 Wine Tasting" with Doug. Almost every visit included a cheese board with brie and jelly. Leighann started working at The Market from the very beginning, our Saturday veteran, in more than one way. She was always a salesperson, and you could bet that you would see her in the morning on Facebook, big smile, showing some wine or cheese that you needed to stop down to get. For her birthday, we didn't serve the usual cake; she preferred the brie with charcoal crackers.

It is the most prized cheese in France, created by monks prior to the eighth century. Creamy like butter, it is covered in an edible white bloomy rind. You will find the texture of americanized brie to be firmer; since it is pasteurized while young, it will never really age. This does, however, make it easier to cook with. Brie is so versatile, it can be used for sweet and savory dishes, so I've given you examples of both.

Versatile Brie

Want to make your cream soups more luxurious? The addition of brie not only helps to create an ultra-creamy texture but also deepens the flavor.

strawberry brie french toast with pink peppercorn cream

½ pound fresh strawberries, quartered if small, sliced if large
1 tablespoon sugar
1 tablespoon balsamic glaze
1 tablespoon minced fresh mint
1 teaspoon crushed pink peppercorns
½ teaspoon vanilla extract
1 jumbo egg
½ cup milk
¼ teaspoon ground cinnamon
1 teaspoon sugar
4 slices thick-cut baguette, angle sliced
¼ cup chilled heavy cream
6 ounces brie, sliced

Mix the strawberries, sugar, balsamic, and mint in a bowl and allow to sit at room temperature.

Soak the crushed peppercorns in the vanilla.

Whisk together the egg, milk, cinnamon, and sugar. Lay the bread in the egg mixture, allowing it to soak up all liquids on only one side.

Whip the cream with the peppercorn vanilla until stiff peaks.

Melt butter on a griddle, lay the soaked bread slices egg-side-down, and put brie slices on two slices of the bread. Once the cheese has melted, put one spoonful of the strawberries on top.

Cook until golden brown, place the other two slices of bread on top to form a sandwich.

Spread a large dollop of whipped cream on each plate and put one of the sandwiches down.

Garnish with additional balsamic and strawberries.

Serves 2

mushroom brie soup

1 teaspoon truffle oil
8 slices thick peppered bacon, finely chopped
1 large yellow onion, minced
6 celery stalks, minced
4 garlic cloves, minced
2 tablespoons thyme
1½ pounds mushrooms, sliced (I use a variety of mushrooms for more complex flavor)
⅛ cup flour
1 cup pinot noir
1 tablespoon worcestershire sauce
1 quart pork stock
2 pounds french brie (remove rind if not snowy white)
4 ounces morel-leek jack cheese, shredded
2 cups milk
salt and pepper to taste

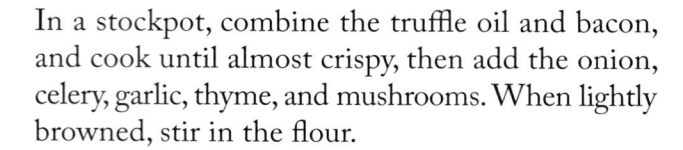

In a stockpot, combine the truffle oil and bacon, and cook until almost crispy, then add the onion, celery, garlic, thyme, and mushrooms. When lightly browned, stir in the flour.

Add the wine and worcestershire, allowing the mushrooms to soak up the liquid. Then add the stock. Allow to simmer for 30 minutes.

In the meantime, blend the brie, jack cheese, and milk in a small pan, on low heat, and cook until melted, stirring until creamy. Slowly add to the stockpot.

Continue to simmer, not too hot, until it all blends and melds together. It should reduce about an inch or more and thicken. Season to taste.

Serves 6 - 8

Sometimes you just feel a bit nostalgic and want to release the inner child in you, and this sandwich accomplishes that. Have a glass of wine with it to be a little naughty!

grilled PBJBrie

2 slices raisin bread
3 ounces cold brie, sliced
2 tablespoons peanut butter
1 tablespoon spicy pepper jelly
1 tablespoon grape jelly

Butter one side of each slice of bread. On medium heat, place the bread butter-side-down. Place a layer of brie on one slice. When the cheese is almost melted, spread peanut butter on the other slice. Mix both jellies together and spoon over the brie. Put the sandwich together, place on a plate with a small bed of greens, a bundle of grapes, and our macNcheese (see page 72).

blueberry brie pie

1 cup sugar
6 tablespoons cornstarch
1 tablespoon rubbed sage
1 lemon, juice and zest
8 cups fresh blueberries
2 tablespoons merlot

2 pie crusts
½ pound brie, sliced into 8 pieces
8 large fresh sage leaves
1 egg, beaten

In a large bowl, mix the sugar, cornstarch, sage, and lemon zest, add the blueberries, drizzle with merlot and lemon juice, and toss to coat the berries.

Pour half of the filling into the bottom pie crust, place the brie slices on top so there is one slice per piece when you cut the pie, then pour in the remaining half of the filling.

Cover with the top crust, crimp the edges, score the crust where the portions will be cut, press sage leaves into the crust between the scores, then brush with egg.

Place on a baking sheet to catch any juice that might drip over the edge. Bake at 375 degrees for 1 hour.

Cool for at least 2 hours before slicing, to allow the filling to set up.

Serves 8

for the love of pies...

Making pie was not one of my strong points, in particular the crust itself. I tried shortening, butter, and lard, and the crusts all turned out tough. Everyone tried to help me with my conundrum. I chilled the dough, added vinegar, changed from a glass pan to metal, still no luck.

Store-bought crusts became my friend. I purposely did a terrible job of crimping the crusts together to make sure people knew the pies were home-made. I have since made headway on my pastry skills but still make my trademark ugly pies.

salted caramel apple pie

¼ cup flour
¼ cup brown sugar
½ teaspoon coarse ground himalayan pink sea salt
1 teaspoon cinnamon
¾ teaspoon nutmeg
8 granny smith apples, cut in ¼-inch slices
1 cup bourbon caramel sauce (you can use my caramel recipe from the bourbon bacon caramel sundae on p. 130 or buy ready-made caramel and stir in bourbon to taste)
2 pie crusts
2 tablespoons melted butter
1 egg, beaten well

In a large bowl, mix the flour, sugar, salt, and spices, add the apple slices, and toss until the apples are well coated. Drizzle ½ of the caramel over the apples, tossing as you go.

Layer the apples into one of the unbaked pie shells (they will stack high). Pour the melted butter on top. Place your second pie shell on top, crimping the edges to seal. Brush the crust with egg.

Bake in a 375-degree oven until golden-brown, approximately 35 minutes. While the pie is still hot, slowly brush the other half of the caramel over the entire pie, including the edges. Serve with ice cream or whipped cream.

Serves 8

American Pie

There are many tales as to how the phrase "as American as apple pie" was born, but behind them all is the symbolism of love. The pie shows how ingredients from different cultures can come together to form something new, and isn't that what America is supposed to be all about?

sweet potato pecan pie

3 cups mashed sweet potatoes
4 tablespoons butter
5 eggs
1 cup brown sugar
¾ teaspoon nutmeg
¼ teaspoon salt
4 tablespoons bourbon
2 teaspoons vanilla
1 cup milk
1 pie crust, chilled
2 cups pecan pieces
½ cup brown sugar
1 tablespoon bourbon
3 tablespoons maple syrup
⅛ teaspoon sea salt

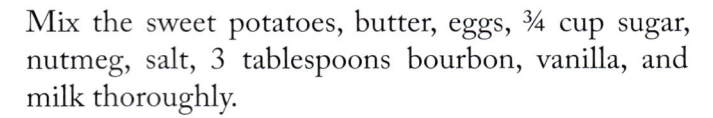

Mix the sweet potatoes, butter, eggs, ¾ cup sugar, nutmeg, salt, 3 tablespoons bourbon, vanilla, and milk thoroughly.

Take the pie crust out of the refrigerator, lay it on a floured surface and roll out into a circle, then lay it in a pie pan. Crimp the edges on the rim, then randomly pierce the dough with a fork to allow steam to escape while baking. Bake in a preheated 375-degree oven just till lightly golden brown.

Take the warm crust out of the oven and pour your filling into it, then return to the oven until the center jiggles like Jell-o, approximately 40 minutes.

While the pie cooks, mix the pecan pieces, the remaining brown sugar and bourbon, and the sea salt to make the topping.

Once the pie is jiggly, take it out of the oven and lightly press the pecan topping over the entire top of the pie, then return it to the oven to bake for another 10–15 minutes to caramelize the sugar.

Serves 8

finally worked pie crust

1½ cups all-purpose flour
½ teaspoon salt
1 tablespoon sugar
10 tablespoons unsalted butter, cut into small pieces and frozen for 15 minutes
¾ tablespoon sherry cider vinegar, chilled
⅛ cup water, chilled

Mix the flour, salt, and sugar, then add the butter, mixing with a fork until pea-sized crumbs form.

Add the vinegar and water, mixing until the dough just holds together; if it is still crumbly, add another tablespoon of ice water but don't over mix.

Put the dough onto a lightly floured surface and knead a few times to form into two flattened balls, then cover with plastic wrap and refrigerate while making the filling.

rhubarb tarragon pie

1 cup sugar
⅓ cup cornstarch
2 tablespoons minced fresh tarragon (save 8 large leaves for garnish)
1 orange, zest and juice
2 pounds rhubarb, thickly sliced
2 tablespoons butter, cut into small chunks
2 pie crusts
1 egg, beaten

In a large bowl, mix the sugar, cornstarch, tarragon, and orange zest, add the rhubarb, drizzle with orange juice, and toss to coat the rhubarb. Pour the filling into the bottom pie crust.

Cover with the top crust, crimp the edges, score the crust where the portions will be cut, press tarragon leaves into the crust between the scores, then brush with egg.

Place the pie on a baking sheet to catch any juice that might drip over the edge, and bake at 375 degrees for one hour.

Cool for at least 2 hours, to allow the filling to set up before slicing.

Serves 8

we all have favorites...

Some of the best-loved items from Food n' Fermentations, such as the lemon chicken, the cranberry turkey sandwich, and the tomato soup, continued to hold their place on our new, ever-changing menu. New champions emerged. Some dishes remained on the menu but went through metamorphosis as the years passed. But only one item held its place from the beginning to the end, with no change, and that was our bourbon caramel bacon sundae. One would come out into the dining room and like a chain reaction, others had to order it also.

bourbon caramel bacon sundae

3 slices bacon
3 scoops salted caramel ice cream
¼ cup bourbon caramel sauce
⅛ cup candied walnuts

Dice the bacon while frozen; it is easier to cut uniformly. Cook it until it's just crispy, then place on a paper towel to dab off extra grease.

Put 2 scoops of ice cream in a rocks glass and tamp down. Top with a thick layer of caramel sauce and two thirds of the bacon. Place one more scoop of ice cream on top. Poke in candied walnuts. Place the remaining bacon on top. Drape the entire thing in caramel.

candied walnuts

3 cups sugar
3 tablespoons cinnamon
1 tablespoon sea salt
2 egg whites
2 pounds whole walnuts

Combine the sugar, cinnamon, and salt.

Whisk the egg whites until foamy. Fold in the walnuts. Slowly sprinkle in the sugar mixture, tossing to coat the nuts completely.

Spread them out in a single layer on a parchment-lined baking sheet. Bake at 350 degrees until golden brown, about 12 minutes; rotate the pan in the oven after the first 6 minutes to ensure even cooking.

bourbon caramel sauce

2 cups packed brown sugar
⅔ cup unsalted butter, cut in pieces
1 cup heavy cream
½ tablespoon coarse ground himalayan pink sea salt
¼ cup bourbon

Melt the sugar in a high-sided saucepan on medium heat, stirring constantly so it doesn't burn. Once it starts to bubble, whisk in the butter. Once blended, slowly pour in the cream; be careful, it will foam up. Once it is creamy, take it off heat; the caramel will thicken more as it cools.

Once it is at room temperature, fold in the salt and bourbon.

Makes 2 cups

The simplest, yet most requested, plate, was the caprese salad. This is the epitome of a recipe that showcases the importance of quality ingredients. We would change the presentation and preparation each season to allow the tomato to be at its best. An understanding of the different traits of the components in a dish such as this is imperative to its success. Here I share four different ways to enjoy a caprese.

The main ingredient, the tomato, is the most grown vegetable in the world. Gardeners compare notes, their neighbors wait for the glut of crops, and chefs are first in line at the local farmers market. This summer gem is so much more than a salad and sandwich garnish. Cooked into sauces as a source of umami or being the acidic star on its own, I find it to be a rock star in the kitchen.

When the seed catalogs arrive, it gets increasingly difficult to select from all the tomato varieties that are available. With the popularity of heirlooms, the flavor profiles have risen to new levels. Pick the perfect tomato for what you'll be using it for, and you'll be awarded with the ultimate delicious dish.

Cherry, grape, and pear tomatoes are the perfect choice for snacking. I have a potted plant on the patio for quick access to satisfy sudden hunger pangs. They tend to be sweeter and have thicker skins than other tomatoes, so when they're tossed into a salad or lightly sautéed, they will give you a fun burst of flavor. Grill lovers should put them on a skewer with halloumi cheese.

winter potted caprese

10 cherry tomatoes
6 bocconcini mozzarella
6 basil leaves, torn in large pieces
2 tablespoons extra virgin olive oil
himalayan pink sea salt
balsamic glaze
basil crystals

Using a stovetop cast iron griddle pan, lightly char the tomatoes on all sides; do not overcook. Put in a bowl and add the mozzarella and basil. Toss with olive oil, sprinkle with salt. You can serve this on a plate, but we presented it in a jar. Drizzle with balsamic and sprinkle with basil crystals. Serve with toasted baguette slices.

Serves 1

On a hot summer night, enjoying a chilled caprese martini while touring the gardens is beyond refreshing. It's an appetizer and cocktail all in one!

caprese martini

drop of balsamic glaze
¼ teaspoon basil crystals
3 ounces Moletto gin
¼ teaspoon basil-infused vinegar
¼ teaspoon dry vermouth
4 basil leaves
2 cherry tomatoes
2 bocconcini mozzarella balls or cut squares of mozzarella

Chill a martini glass in the freezer.

In the bottom of the chilled glass, place the one drop of balsamic glaze and the basil crystals. Put ice in a cocktail shaker and add the gin, vinegar, vermouth, and 2 of the basil leaves. Shake vigorously, strain into the martini glass, and garnish with a skewer of the tomatoes, the remaining basil leaves, and the mozzarella.

Serves 1

Moletto Gin

Moletto gin is from the Veneto region in Italy. Select mixed grains are distilled in copper stills, then separate infusions of juniper berries, from the Alps and from the Mediterranean coast, are blended in. But what makes this special gin completely different is the addition of ripe tomatoes, which gives it a unique taste and the distinct aroma of tomato leaves.

Plum and roma tomatoes are meaty with few seeds, cooking down to beautiful sauces. If you have an aversion to the seedy pulp of tomatoes, this variety will give you the opportunity to enjoy a BLT without the textural disfavor. In this category lies the San Marzano. During the winter, this is my go-to tomato, sold canned in specialty grocery stores. This particular tomato is grown in a relatively small region between Naples and Salerno and is guarded by Designation of Origin, the same as parmigiano reggiano and champagne. The name of these items are protected by their country or region because the quality and characteristics cannot be duplicated in any other geographical location. The seed is available and is grown in other areas and fraudulently sold as San Marzano, so beware when shopping; remember, terroir makes a difference.

Beefsteaks, the juicy giants of the tomato world, are the last ones to ripen. One slice will cover any burger or sandwich. They have a higher water content and a milder flavor, so are best eaten raw and not used for sauce. They were delicious on our caprese grilled cheese sandwich.

caprese grilled cheese

On one piece of the bread, press shredded parmigiano onto the buttered side to coat, then place cheese-side-down on a heated griddle. Place a second slice of bread butter-side-down on the griddle. On one piece of bread, lay down mozzarella slices. On the other slice, spread 1 spoonful of pesto and top with tomato slices. Slowly cook until the mozzarella is melted and the parmigiano has turned into a golden-brown crust. Lay the parm-crusted bread on top and drizzle with balsamic.

Serves 1

2 slices of sourdough bread, buttered on one side
3 tablespoons shredded parmigiano reggiano
4 ounces fresh mozzarella, sliced
2 tablespoons basil pesto
2 beefsteak tomato slices
balsamic glaze

On the Vine, also known as hothouse tomatoes, have a very mild tomato flavor and overly thick skin. I would have to be desperate to use these; tomatoes are just best used during the growing season.

Heirlooms are grown from saved seeds at least fifty years old. Since they are not bred to be perfect, they are not always the prettiest tomatoes, but their intense flavor and unique colors make up for it. Most have a soft texture, so handle with care. I have found that the darker the color, the more acidic they are. The striped varieties are very fruity and sweet; the black varieties have a smoky rich flavor. If the acidity in tomatoes bother you, try the yellow or green heirlooms. This is the tomato I prefer to use for my summer caprese.

Except for marinara, the caprese salad is the first thing most people think of when you talk about tomatoes. In our area, the anticipation of the first summer-ripened tomato is palpable! The Market's stacked caprese sold by the hundreds each week, depleting all the house-grown and farm-delivered tomatoes quickly. You would see Doug hitting the farmers market early on Saturday mornings.

summer caprese salad

8 large basil leaves
4 heirloom tomato slices, preferably both yellow and red
3 slices fresh mozzarella
2 tablespoons extra virgin olive oil
1 tablespoon balsamic glaze
½ tablespoon basil crystals
himalayan pink sea salt

Layer the basil, tomatoes, and mozzarella.

Drizzle with olive oil and balsamic, top with basil crystals, and sprinkle with salt.

Story of a Salad

The caprese salad was named after the island of Capri, where it is believed to have originated in the 1920s. The story goes that at a dinner reception held at the Hotel Quisisana it was served in tribute to Italy, incorporating the colors of the flag. After the favorable response, the dish was added to the hotel's menu.

Garden tomato varieties abound, from early girls to big boys, yellow, green, or red. The most versatile of all varieties, they can be enjoyed raw or cooked in any matter of preparation. A basic rule of thumb is the smaller the tomato, the sweeter it will be. Speaking of sweetness, do not be afraid to use tomatoes in dessert recipes.

I prepared a baked tomato dessert for one of our wine dinners. Dave and Lana Mounts, from Mounts Family Winery in Dry Creek Valley, were our hosts. Paired with their Grenache, it was a huge hit. But having Lana say that this was the best dessert she ever had, and how amazingly it paired with their wine, was the greatest of all compliments!

fruit stuffed baked tomato with ice cream

¾ cup golden raisins
½ cup dried figs, chopped
1 cup grenache wine, heated
½ cup brown sugar
1 tablespoon melted butter
4 tomatoes, stem on
4 large scoops vanilla bean ice cream
¼ cup pepitas

Soak the raisins and figs in the hot wine for 1 hour to plump. Drain.

Mix the fruit with the brown sugar and butter.

Cut the tomato tops off and scoop out the centers. Stuff with the fruit filling.

Bake in a 350-degree oven for 15 minutes.

Put on a plate, place a scoop of ice cream on top, and sprinkle with pepitas.

Lay the top of a tomato on a lid.

Serves 4

Green tomatoes are both a varietal and an under-ripe red tomato. A true green tomato has stripes or other color variations, is soft to the touch, and will taste like a red tomato. Unripe tomatoes are pale green all over, feel solid, and have a tart flavor. Both are edible delights.

Fried green tomatoes, a southern delicacy, are what most people think of when they look at that pile of tomatoes they rescued from the vine before the first frost hit. Pickled, sweet or savory, they can be used in so many dishes. These are two of my favorites.

green tomato parsnip soup with scallops

1 small yellow onion, chopped
1 pound parsnips, peeled and chopped finely
2 pounds green tomatoes, chopped
1 pear, cored and chopped
4 cups vegetable broth
1 small handful arugula
1 tablespoon garlic powder
1 tablespoon minced fresh basil
1 tablespoon dill weed
1 teaspoon white pepper
1 tablespoon celery salt
2 cups heavy cream
1 pound bay scallops, lightly sautéed in butter
3 green onions, diced

In a stockpot, sauté the onions in olive oil until translucent, then add the parsnips, green tomatoes, and pear.

Add half of the vegetable broth and simmer until the vegetables are soft. Add the arugula and cook until wilted.

Puree with an immersion blender.

Add the remaining stock, the spices, and the cream. Simmer until flavors are blended.

Garnish with warm scallops and minced green onion.

Serves 8

green tomato pie

½ cup golden raisins
¼ cup riesling wine, heated
¾ cup sugar
¼ cup flour
½ teaspoon cinnamon
1 teaspoon nutmeg
4 cups thinly sliced green tomatoes
2 pie crusts
3 tablespoons butter
1 egg, whipped

Soak the raisins in the heated riesling for an hour.

Combine the sugar, flour, cinnamon, and nutmeg, then add the tomatoes, toss to coat, and fold in the raisins and the wine not soaked in by them.

Put the filling in the bottom crust, dot with butter, lay on the top crust, and seal the edges.

Brush the top of the crust with whipped egg.

Bake at 350 degrees for 1 hour.

Serves 8

Basil is the tomato's best friend in the garden; the aroma confuses the harmful insects, keeping them away from the fruit. Their love affair continues into the kitchen. The herb's sweet and peppery flavor cuts the acidity and brings out the tomato's sweetness. Most recipes call for sweet basil, but there are other varieties, such as lemon, thai, and cinnamon. They allow for creativity and add a touch of unexpected flavor to your dish or cocktail.

I recommend using fresh whenever possible; dried basil has a different taste, bringing out more of a licorice flavor. Fresh basil has a short shelf life, making it a bit expensive in the grocery store, so grow your own. During the winter, a pot on your sunny windowsill or an AeroGarden will keep you happily harvesting for all your basil needs. The plants grow quickly and like to be pinched back often.

If you find yourself with extra, there are a couple of ways to preserve your precious leaves. Chop them and pack them into ice cube trays, covered with tomato juice or water. Once frozen, toss the cubes into a ziplock bag for use in soup or sauces at a later time. Another option is to make pesto, a raw sauce originating from Genoa, Italy. It is so popular there, the villagers have been heard to say, "The first thing we give to a baby, after milk, is pesto."

our basil pesto

4 tablespoon marcona almonds
½ teaspoon sea salt
3 garlic cloves, peeled
½ teaspoon lemon juice
2 cups basil leaves, torn into pieces
½ cup olive oil
¼ cup shredded parmigiano reggiano
¼ cup shredded pecorino

You can use a food processor, but using a mortar and pestle results in a chunkier texture and releases the oil for a more fragrant mixture. Plus, there is honestly a primal satisfaction derived from grinding like you're in the Stone Age, appreciating the process, not rushing through it.

So put the nuts, salt, and garlic cloves in the mortar. Using the pestle, pound and scrape around the sides until it's a smooth paste. Add the lemon juice and ¼ of the basil, working it into the mixture, then continue adding and mixing until all 2 cups of the basil have been blended in.

Transfer the basil paste to a bowl. Slowly begin to stir the oil into the basil paste until well blended. Fold in the cheese. Store in a jar topped with a thin layer of olive oil to seal, then refrigerate.

Makes 1 cup

Pestle and Pesto

Both pestle and pesto come from the Italian verb pestare, meaning to crush, which makes sense since basil should be torn by hand and not cut with a knife. When metal touches it, the leaves will darken quicker and can take on a metallic taste. According to an age-old superstition, scorpions will rise from it if cut, so who wants to test that theory?!

The "magic" ingredient that made our caprese salad so unique was basil crystals. They added that crunchy texture and a kiss of basil sweetness. We purchased them, but you can make your own at home.

basil crystals

1 cup sugar
½ cup chopped fresh basil

In a food processor, pulse the sugar and basil until they stick together. Spread a thin layer of the mixture on a piece of parchment paper, then put it in the oven at the lowest temperature setting and allow it to dry for a day. Be sure to check on the crystals and stir gently to break up the sugar. Once completely dry, store the crystals in a jar in a dark, dry cupboard.

So, have you ever had an argument about whether a tomato and eggplant is a vegetable? Technically, you are correct either way. Botanically they are both fruit, but since they are savory in flavor, they are classified as vegetables. Either way, culinarily, they both can be prepared in savory or dessert dishes. Eggplant has a bland flavor with a little bitterness in the skin. Like a sponge, it takes in the flavor of the other ingredients it's cooked with.

I enjoy growing my own eggplants. They have beautiful purple flowers that give way to quick-growing fruit. The skin gets tougher the longer they are off the vine, so I prefer to go from garden to griddle. Many people peel them before cooking, but you are then removing the most nutritious part.

There are many heirloom varieties, white to dark purple in color, skinny to plump. Other than the appearance, there is truly little difference between them. However, the Japanese eggplant, long and slender, does have a creamier consistency when cooked. They are the most popular variety for making baba ganoush, but my favorite way to use them is as a substitute for hot dogs. Rub the eggplant with olive oil, grill, put in a bakery bun, and top with tomato relish. Give it a try, you won't be disappointed!

The globe and Italian varieties are the most commonly used. Even though the Spaniards were the ones that brought the crop to America, most of us think of them as Italian, especially in the Italian dish of eggplant parmigiano.

eggplant parmigiano

Doug anxiously awaits the cutting of the first glorious purple eggplant. Eggplant parmigiano is one of his favorite dishes. Each time I prepare it, even though it changes, depending on what the garden tempts me with, he says it is the best ever. So, I will share version 26 with you. Just like my lasagna, I have never measured and written down a recipe. I will simply walk you through it, highlighting the ingredients you need. These are dishes that allow for freedom and creativity.

It all starts in my garden. If you don't have a green thumb, head to your local farmers market or a grocer who keeps fresh produce. Gather a medium sized **eggplant**, (not too soft, should have shiny skin), a few **tomatoes**, a **fennel** bulb, chives or yellow **onion**, bulb **garlic**, and fresh **herbs** (basil, thyme, and oregano).

Start your grill while preparing the veggies. This step is optional, but a bit of grilled veggie taste adds to the balance of sweet and bitter. Cut the fronds off the fennel bulb, quarter the onion, and core the tomatoes. Along with the bulb of garlic, rub them all with a little olive oil and throw them on the top shelf of the grill.

While they cook, slice the eggplant into rounds, about an inch thick. Coat the slices in beaten **egg**, then a mixture of equal parts of **flour** and **cornmeal.** Generously sprinkle with **sea salt** and **pepper.** Sauté in olive oil until golden brown on both sides. Let cool. Perfect timing to go out and turn your veggies on the grill.

Continue prepping by mincing the herbs, slicing **mozzarella**, and finely grating **parmigiano reggiano.** I mixed the parm with a little fresh **cream** and reduced it into a thick alfredo-style sauce, but this is optional.

Rescue the grilled veggies, thinly slice the fennel and onion. Crush the tomatoes and peeled garlic together. Now the fun begins . . . let's assemble it.

Spray or lightly oil the baking dish (I prefer glass, it bakes evenly and you can peek at the action as it cooks). Starting with the eggplant rounds, you will then layer the tomato, fennel, and onion. Finish with one more layer of eggplant. Then carefully spoon your crushed tomato and garlic over the top, followed by spoonfuls of the parm cream. Finish with mozzarella garnished with herbs and a random sprinkling of grated parmigiano.

Bake until bubbly and golden. Don't overcook; you want the eggplant to still have texture and to be able to reheat the leftovers without that "burnt" flavor. Let it sit for a few minutes to allow it to set up before serving, perfect timing to open a bottle of wine and savor your labor.

To make it look special, once plated, I topped the dish with a drizzle of balsamic glaze and some microgreens.

A more unusual way to serve eggplant is in one of my favorite desserts to make in the late summer when it is plentiful . . . always a surprise when you tell your guests what it's made with!

eggplant chocolate torte

1¼ cups sugar
¾ teaspoon cinnamon
2 oranges, zested
2 eggplants, sliced lengthwise about ¼-inch thick
1 cup flour
8 ounces bittersweet chocolate chips
1 cup heavy whipping cream
1¼ cup ricotta, press extra liquid out in strainer
1½ ounces ginger snap cookies, crushed
2 ounces sliced almonds
2 ounces candied orange peel, chopped
2 large eggs, lightly beaten

Prepare eggplant: Mix 1 cup of the sugar, the cinnamon, and the orange zest and spread on a plate. Lightly dust the eggplant slices in flour and fry in olive oil until golden brown on both sides, then remove from the oil, press each slice in the sugar mix, and place it on a tray lined with paper towels.

Chocolate sauce: Put the chocolate in a small metal mixing bowl. Heat the whipping cream until it just comes to a boil, then pour over the chocolate, gently stirring until melted. Let it cool down.

Ricotta filling: Blend the ricotta, the remaining ¼ cup sugar, the cookie crumbs, almonds, and candied orange peel in a bowl, fold in the eggs, and set aside.

Preheat the oven to 375 degrees and butter a 9 X 9 baking dish.

Building it: Lay the eggplant slices on the bottom and sides of the baking pan like a pie crust, so the slices are draping over the sides of the dish. Spread one half of the filling over the eggplant, then spread half of the chocolate sauce. Do another layer of eggplant, filling, and chocolate sauce. Put down another layer of eggplant, then fold the eggplant draped over the sides of the dish back over the dessert and press lightly to seal and even the layers.

Bake for 20–30 minutes. Allow it to cool down before slicing into portions. Serve with a drizzle of chocolate syrup and softened espresso ice cream.

Serves 12

Most everyone loves garlic, but have you tried black garlic? When I first saw it as a secret ingredient on the Food Network show Chopped, I immediately began searching out ways to get it. After a bit of sticker shock, I hesitantly ordered it and awaited its arrival. As soon as we opened the box, a wonderfully sweet aroma of molasses was released. The black clove pressed out from the skin easily. It was sticky, soft, and had a flavor like aged balsamic or saba. I knew that I was going to enjoy playing with this newfound ingredient.

Black garlic is simply regular garlic that undergoes a special process of aging. The entire bulb is held at a regulated temperature and humidity for one to three months. This causes the enzymes that make garlic pungent to break down. The reaction that turns it dark can be compared to what happens when you sear meat or sauté onions.

There are many articles available on making your own black garlic at home using your ricer or slow cooker. If you opt to do this, realize that the room will reek of garlic throughout the process. Pricing and availability have improved since I first started using it. But be wary if the price seems too low to believe, because there is a difference in quality. You can find black garlic in whole bulbs, peeled cloves, or powdered.

beet and black garlic soup with beetgreen pesto and ginger crème

3 pounds beets with greens
2 red onions
3 tablespoons olive oil
1 tablespoon balsamic glaze
1 tablespoon himalayan pink sea salt
6 cups beef or vegetable broth
2 tablespoons thyme
2 tablespoons dill weed
6 black garlic cloves, peeled
salt and pepper
beetgreen pesto
ginger crème

Peel and quarter the beets, saving the greens for the pesto.

Peel the onions and cut in half.

Place the onions and beets in a bowl and toss with the olive oil, balsamic, and sea salt. Place on a baking sheet and roast until the beets can be pierced with a fork, about 1 hour.

Pour the broth, thyme, dill, and black garlic into a stockpot. Add the roasted beets and onions. Using an immersion blender to puree until smooth. Season to taste with salt and pepper, and simmer for about 20 minutes or until reduced to desired thickness.

Ladle into a serving bowl or cup. Top with pesto and ginger cream. Garnish with chives or green onions.

Serves 8

beetgreen pesto

¼ cup shelled pistachios
3 cups chopped beet greens
½ teaspoon minced garlic
juice and zest of 1 orange
¼ cup extra virgin olive oil
salt to taste

Pulse the pistachios in a food processor, then add the beet greens, garlic, and orange. Slowly incorporate the olive oil. Salt to taste.

Makes 1 pint

ginger crème

1 cup heavy cream
1 tablespoon ground ginger

Blend together on high speed until stiff peaks begin to form.

black garlic prime rib sandwich

2 tablespoons black garlic aioli (see recipe below)
1 black sesame seed brioche bun, toasted
4 ounces prime rib, cooked to medium-rare, thinly sliced, warmed before serving
3 ounces sauteed local oyster mushrooms
pickled red onion
baby arugula

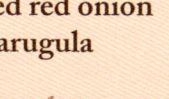

Spread a thick layer of aioli on the bun bottom. Stack the prime rib, topped with mushrooms, then red onion and arugula. Spread another thin layer of aioli on the top bun.

black garlic aioli

5 black garlic cloves
1 roasted garlic clove
½ teaspoon lemon juice
½ teaspoon black garlic shoyu
¼ teaspoon salt
1 egg yolk
1 teaspoon sesame oil
½ cup olive oil

In a blender, mix the garlic, lemon juice, shoyu, and salt into a paste.

Add the egg yolk, blending until smooth.

Slowly pour in the oil until the mixture emulsifies into a thick, creamy aioli.

Makes ¾ cup

Shoyu

There are Chinese and Japanese soy sauces. Shoyu is a Japanese soy sauce naturally fermented with only four ingredients: soybean, wheat, water, and salt. Chinese soy sauce can have upward of a dozen different ingredients, including caramel coloring. Shoyu will be lighter in color and density, with a sweeter, rich flavor. Chinese soy sauce is thicker and dark in color, with a sharp, salty bite.

One of the things I love to grow in my garden is a large variety of peppers. Not only are they beautiful plants, but the flavor and heat level are unique to each variety. Shishito peppers are gaining popularity as a quick and easy appetizer sure to bring excitement to the party as your guests take the chance of getting that one out of ten that is spicy!

blistered black garlic shishito pepper

1 pound shishito peppers
2 cups black garlic shoyu
5 tablespoons sesame oil
2 tablespoons minced fresh ginger root
4 green onions, thinly sliced
1 teaspoon crushed pink peppercorns
2 tablespoons white sesame seed
1 tablespoon olive oil

Keep your peppers whole, including the stem. Make sure they are perfectly dry, or they will spatter hot oil all over!

Stir together the shoyu and sesame oil until well blended. Add the ginger, green onions, peppercorns, and sesame seeds.

Heat 1 tablespoon of olive oil in a wok or flat pan. When it's hot, lay your peppers in the pan but do not overcrowd; you'll want to turn and blister both sides.

Put the hot peppers in a bowl, tossing lightly with a small portion of the shoyu mix, just enough to glaze. Pour the remaining shoyu mix into dipping cups on your serving plates.

To enjoy, pick up the pepper by the stem, dip it into the shoyu cup, and bite it off at the stem.

Serves 6

Another ingredient that deserves understanding is the truffle, a rare fungus that grows under the cover of mainly oak trees in Italy and France. In the wild, they are harvested by trained foragers that use pigs or dogs to sniff them out. They are found growing in other areas, and are being commercially farmed in the United States, but in my opinion, these do not yield near the flavor as the wild white and black truffle of Europe.

Black truffles can be found for up to nine months out of the year, making them more readily available and at a much lower price than the rare white truffle. They have a stronger taste, comparable to a dry-cured black olive. Their earthy aromas, especially after being released by heat, can be quite heady. When purchasing fresh or processed, you will see three different classifications.

- Black winter truffles are found wild roughly from November to February. They do grow in other countries, but the best of the best come from the Périgord region of France. They have the darkest color and the strongest flavor of all black truffles.

- Burgundy truffles are the most widely grown, found in many countries, from Sweden to the northern parts of Africa. They have more of a brown color than black truffles and are milder in flavor, more nutty than earthy.

- Summer truffles are the most commonly found truffle across Europe, available from May through September. They are black on the outside but have a pale, very firm center. These will be the least expensive truffles, but you will get what you pay for.

truffle grilled cheese

2 slices sourdough bread, buttered on one side
3 tablespoons shredded parmigiano reggiano
2 tablespoons black truffle tapenade
4 ounces taleggio, thickly sliced
truffle zest

Press shredded parmigiano onto the buttered side to coat one piece of bread, then place cheese-side-down on a heated griddle, and spread a thin layer of tapenade on top. Place a second slice of bread buttered-side-down on the griddle and lay the cheese slices on top. Cook until the parmigiano has turned into a golden-brown crust and the cheese just starts to melt. If you cook it for too long, the cheese will melt away. Place the sandwich on a plate with the parm-crusted side up. Dust with truffle zest. Serve with tomato soup.

Serves 1

black truffle tapenade

¾ cup olive oil
1 tablespoon minced garlic
½ cup thinly sliced oyster mushrooms
1 teaspoon thyme
1 tablespoon capers
2 white anchovy filets, minced
¼ cup minced black olives
3 ounces black truffle peelings
½ teaspoon truffle oil
1 teaspoon lemon juice
salt and pepper to taste

In a saucepan, heat the olive oil, add the garlic, mushrooms, and thyme, and sauté just until the mushrooms are sweaty and soft. Take off heat and fold in the remaining ingredients. If dry, add additional olive oil. Allow to cool.

Makes 1 ½ cups

Truffle Zest

The Sabatino truffle zest we used is a blend of powdered black truffle and carob. It was on Oprah's list of favorite things, and after trying it, I added it to mine. Used for finishing dishes, it gives you that truffle aroma and light flavor. Try sprinkling it on your popcorn or french fried potatoes!

I would be remiss if I didn't add the recipe for my truffle chips after promising my friend Kelly!

truffle parmigiano chips

2 pounds russet potatoes
4 cups canola oil
6 tablespoons finely grated parmigiano reggiano
1 tablespoon grated sap sago cheese
1 teaspoon truffle oil
1 tablespoon truffle zest
salt and pepper to taste

Using a mandolin, slice the potatoes as thin as possible, and place in a large bowl of salted ice water for 15 minutes. Then lay the slices out on paper towels to dry completely.

Add the potatoes to 350-degree oil in batches and cook until lightly golden and crispy.

Place in a large bowl and toss with the cheeses, truffle oil, truffle zest, salt and pepper.

Serve immediately.

Serves 8

truffled macNcheese

1½ pounds macaroni
½ pound truffle gouda, grated
¼ pound champignon mushroom brie, include the bloom rind if still snowy white
¼ pound taleggio
2 cups cheddar cheese sauce
2 teaspoons truffle oil
2½ cups milk
6 green onions, small diced

¼ pound feta, crumbled
¼ pound fresh mozzarella, torn in pieces
3 ounces black truffle peelings (reserve some for garnish)
¼ cup pepper supreme
1 pound boschetto al tartufo, sliced into a circles
¾ cup bread crumbs
truffle zest

Cook the macaroni in salted boiling water until al dente, drain, and rinse with cool water.

In a saucepan, melt the gouda, brie, taleggio, cheddar cheese sauce, truffle oil, and milk until smooth, stirring often.

Place the noodles in a large bowl. Pour the hot cheese sauce over them. Add pepper supreme, green onions, feta, and mozzarella, stirring gently. Add additional milk if needed. Gently fold in the truffle peelings.

To serve, heap macNcheese into mini cast iron pans. Cover with a slice of boschetto and top with breadcrumbs. Bake at 400 degrees until the cheese is melted and bubbly, about 20 minutes.

Garnish with additional truffle peelings and dust with truffle zest.

Serve with a toasted baguette and a cup of tomato soup

Serves 8 - 10

White truffles are the gems of the earth, rarer than any other edible root, tuber, or mushroom. They are found in the town of Alba and the surrounding area of the Piedmont region of northern Italy only during October through December. Looking like little potatoes, they have an indescribable flavor, a woodsy, minerally pungency. The aroma released from them has an intense earthiness not unlike crushed garlic. They say this truffle may have aphrodisiac traits; I believe anyone would be amorous after being treated to something that is worth over $5,000 per pound.

white truffle bluenose bass with cassoulet

½ cup white wine
½ cup vegetable broth
2 bay leaves
½ tablespoon thyme
1 teaspoon crushed pink peppercorns
2 tablespoons white truffle butter
4 (4–6 ounce) pieces bluenose bass, skinless
cassoulet (see recipe below)
knob of fresh white truffle
salt and pepper to taste

Combine the wine, broth, herbs, and butter in a fry pan and bring to a boil.

Add the fish pieces, lower the heat to a low simmer, and cover.

Poach for about 10 minutes, depending on the thickness. The color will be opaque. Remove the fish.

Reduce the poaching liquid to glaze.

To serve, spoon the cassoulet into the middle of a serving dish. Top with a piece of fish. Thinly slice the truffle and place a couple of pieces on top of the fish, lightly pressing it into the meat. Lightly spoon a little poaching liquid over top. Dust with a little salt and pepper. Add more truffle slices as wanted.

Serves 4

cassoulet

2 cups dried white beans
1 tablespoon salt
6 bay leaves
¼ cup duck fat
½ pound bacon, finely chopped
1 red pepper, minced
1 green pepper, minced
1 yellow onion, diced
1 tablespoon minced garlic
2 tablespoons tomato paste
3 cup vegetable or chicken stock
2 tablespoons black truffle pieces
½ tablespoon cracked black pepper
1 tablespoon thyme
2 sprigs fresh rosemary

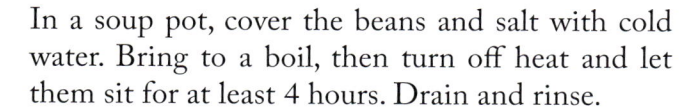

In a soup pot, cover the beans and salt with cold water. Bring to a boil, then turn off heat and let them sit for at least 4 hours. Drain and rinse.

Return the beans to the pot, add the bay leaves, cover with fresh water, and simmer until the beans are just barely tender, about 45 minutes. Strain, saving liquid. Set the beans aside.

In the same pot, heat the duck fat, fry the bacon bits until almost crispy, add the peppers, onion, and garlic, and cook until onions are translucent.

Add the cooked beans, tomato paste, stock, truffle, cracked pepper, thyme, and rosemary, and bring to a boil.

Put the mixture into a casserole dish. Pour in enough saved bean liquid to completely cover the beans.

Bake at 325 degrees for 3 hours. Add more saved bean liquid if needed.

Remove the rosemary stems before serving.

Serves 8

Bluenose Bass

Bluenose bass is found around the offshore reefs of New Zealand. It has sweet, firm yet flaky white flesh. Be careful not to overcook; it will rob you of its silky texture and rich, buttery flavor.

rabbit and white truffle confit on toast

In a small ovenproof pan, melt the duck fat, then add the rabbit, salt, garlic, bay leaves, peppercorns, coriander, thyme, and sage, and bring back to a low simmer.

Place the pot in a 300-degree oven and bake until the meat falls off the bone, about 2 and a half hours.

Strain the fat through a coffee filter. Save ½ cup for use in this recipe; the rest can be stored in the refrigerator.

Remove the meat from the bones, shred, and place in a mixing bowl. Add the green onion, 4 slices of truffle, and the reserved ½ cup duck fat.

With gloved hands, blend all the ingredients well, and if still dry, add a little chicken stock or more of the saved fat. Season to taste with salt and pepper.

Serve on toasted bread spread with truffle butter. Garnish with additional truffle slices and a dusting of smoked paprika.

Serves 6

4 cups duck fat
4 rabbit legs (drummie and thigh)
1 teaspoon pink salt crystals
6 cloves garlic, peeled
6 bay leaves
1 tablespoon crushed pink peppercorns
1 teaspoon coriander seed
1 tablespoon thyme
1 teaspoon rubbed sage
2 green onions, thinly sliced in 2-inch lengths
knob of white truffle
salt and pepper to taste
smoked paprika for garnish

Duck Fat

Duck fat is one of the few fats that can be reused again. Be sure to strain, then store in a jar for up to 3–6 months. It also freezes well. Pull some out to cook your potatoes in, delicious!

giving in to the burger...

One ingredient that I avoided for years was ground beef; apart from an occasional meatloaf or meatballs, you would not find it in my kitchen. Specifically, I did not want a burger on our menu. My desire was to offer foods that you didn't normally see in other eateries. I had an underlying fear that with America's love for burgers, a placement on our menu could turn us into just another burger joint. I would then be forced to bring in ketchup, which anyone who knows me knows is one of my biggest pet peeves!

I did make an exception to the rule for a special event, "Picnic with a Winemaker," that was held out on the patio, hosted by Peter Franus. We had the pleasure of having Peter and his wife Deanne four years before for a tasting, so we were excited to have them back with an opportunity to pair Peter's wines with food.

Our guests would be tasting his new albarino, zinfandel, merlot, and cabernet. The wines were perfect with picnic fare. We served grilled halloumi cheese, fresh-picked tomato and cucumber slices with minced herbs drizzled in olive oil, a napa cabernet burger, and ginger rhubarb cupcakes. The uniqueness of the burger was certainly a topic of the evening's conversations. The pop of the warm grape was a pleasant surprise. I had many requests for the recipe, of which I am now finally sharing.

napa cabernet burger

¼ cup minced red onion
1 cup red grapes
½ tablespoon minced fresh rosemary
1 teaspoon thyme
2 cloves chopped garlic
2 tablespoon cabernet
1½ pounds ground beef
1 teaspoon smoked sea salt
1 tablespoon cracked black pepper
1 tablespoon worcestershire sauce
1 tablespoon bacon fat
1 cup red wine redux sauce (see recipe below)
4 toasted brioche buns

Sauté the onions in olive oil until translucent and lightly browned, then add the grapes, herbs, and garlic. Slowly, add the wine. Cook for a few minutes longer, until the grape peels just begin to burst.

Mix the beef, salt, pepper, worcestershire, and bacon fat. Add the grape-onion mixture.

Divide the meat into 4 patties, making sure the grapes are covered by the meat as much as possible.

Grill or fry the burgers until brown on the bottom, then turn them and brush with some of the wine redux. Continue grilling the burgers until cooked to desired doneness.

Place each burger on a well-toasted bun. Pour wine redux over the top of the burger.

Serves 4

red wine redux sauce

¼ cup butter
2 tablespoons minced garlic
1 tablespoon cracked black pepper
1 cup cabernet wine
1 cup beef stock

In a saucepan, melt the butter, add the garlic to lightly brown, whisk in the remaining ingredients, and bring to a boil. Reduce heat and simmer until the sauce has reduced by half and sticks to a spoon.

Makes 1 cup

Along with a passion for wine, Peter Franus shares my love for creating pleasurable tasting experiences. That evening, he shared stories from years ago, when he was starting as a winemaker. He said something that embodies his guiding principle for making wine. Peter said, *"My greatest satisfaction comes when I see a smile and hear the simple comment, 'this is delicious.' Wine for me is a sensual experience, and my goal is to provide as much pleasure as I can."*

...helped to ease my irrational fear of ...add a burger to the menu at that time, ...ercome my reluctance to compete in the ...ger Battle.

...an annual competition organized by ...lls. After a couple of years, the South ...Foundation became cosponsors. It runs ...th of January. Participating restaurants ...er for the entirety of the competition ...e customers, who rate the burger on its ...bun, along with the presentation and ...ch category is worth up to five points, ...wenty-five possible points.

...ertainly a boon for the restaurants and ...ring a time that would normally be slow due to bad weather. We discovered that the true burger lovers would even come out during a blizzard! Some customers were profoundly serious about it, analyzing each part of the sandwich as if they were forensic investigators. Many just had fun with the competition, leaving lighthearted notes for the chef.

And Chef Greg Springer deserved every bit of the great reviews for his creativity. I believe Cory Meyers from the Argus Leader described the burger better than I can, in his article announcing us as winners of the competition on February 4, 2016.

"The 2016 Downtown Burger Battle winner is not going to come as a surprise to those who tried it. While there were many good burgers this year, and I thoroughly enjoyed chowing my way through them, it was pretty clear that The Market's Market Charcuterie Burger was something special."

He continued on to say, *"The beef and pork belly patty was juicy, wonderfully fatty. I'm now of the opinion that every hamburger patty should be made this way. The in-house cured and smoked peppercorn bacon was phenomenal, and the choice of pepato cheese with peppercorns matched up very well. And the whole seed, pickled mustard? That stuff was insane. Resembling caviar, the pearls of mustard gave the already decadent burger an aura of sophistication. And we've not even touched on the red wine sauce. Clearly I wasn't the only one who loved this burger."*

We sold 547 of these burgers, with an average score of 24.515 out of a possible 25, the highest recorded in the three years DTSF had been hosting this event.

market charcuterie burger

1 pound pork belly
2 pounds ground beef, 80/20
6 slices pepato cheese, cut ¼-inch thick
1 cup red wine redux sauce (see recipe, p. 160)
6 roasted garlic buns with black sesame seeds
12 cooked slices bacon
bread and butter pickles
pickled mustard seed (see recipe below)
micro greens

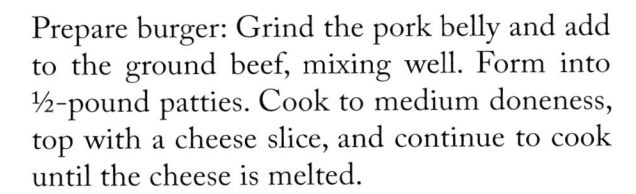

Prepare burger: Grind the pork belly and add to the ground beef, mixing well. Form into ½-pound patties. Cook to medium doneness, top with a cheese slice, and continue to cook until the cheese is melted.

Assemble: Spread a spoonful of redux on a toasted bun bottom, crisscross 2 slices of bacon over it, place the burger over that cheese-side-down, spoon 1 more spoonful of redux on top, layer with pickles, spoon on mustard seed, and finish with micro greens.

Serve with a side of extra wine redux.

Serves 6

pickled mustard seed

2 cups yellow mustard seed
2 cups rice wine vinegar
1½ cups sake
1½ cups water
⅛ teaspoon Colman's dry mustard
1 cup sugar

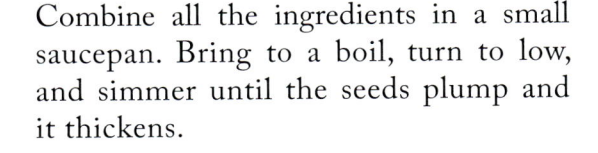

Combine all the ingredients in a small saucepan. Bring to a boil, turn to low, and simmer until the seeds plump and it thickens.

Makes 1 quart

We continued to win the Burger Battle for the next three years, proud to have a four-year run! Each year the number of burgers sold skyrocketed. In our final year we had sold 1,748 for the month. Because of all the requests to continue having a burger past January, we did come up with a compromise.

The third Thursday of the month became the official burger day. Each month we featured a different one; in most cases they were designed to pair with the wine tasting held in the cellar. It was a bustling day oftentimes, with us having to turn customers away because we were full. We had created a monster.

It became difficult for the kitchen and servers to keep up. This day did, however, become a great team-building exercise. I was immensely proud of our staff, watching them help each other out. The girls went back to help prep and the guys helped bring out food. I knew that I would have to eventually give in and just put a burger on the menu. I would not give up on the no ketchup rule though!

We made our burgers from wagyu, lamb, elk, buffalo, and venison. They were 8-ounce patties, thick and juicy. We never skimped on the quality of the ingredients, always the finest of cheese, and we used local produce anytime possible. When I announced that I was writing this book, these were the most requested recipes.

pepper lover's burger

1 poblano pepper
1 jalapeño pepper
1 shishito pepper
1 pound ground wagyu beef
salt and pepper
chili powder
2 thick slices provolone cheese
2 brioche buns, grilled
2 tablespoons shredded pecorino
chipotle aioli (see recipe below)

Char the peppers lightly, then chop in large dice and sauté to soften and rewarm.

Make 2 (8-ounce) patties, season with salt, pepper, and chili powder.

After you flip the burgers, lay down a slice of provolone on top of each and cook to desired doneness.

Spread a thick layer of chipotle aioli on each bottom bun, top with a burger, and place peppers on top.

Garnish with pecorino.

Serves 2

chipotle aioli

1 cup mayonnaise
2 teaspoons lime juice
½ tablespoon garlic salt
2 tablespoons chopped chipotle in adobe sauce

Mix all ingredients.

blt burger

1 pound ground beef
salt and pepper
¼ cup mayo
2 tablespoons chopped basil
1 teaspoon white balsamic
2 brioche buns
spring greens
bacon tomato jam (see recipe below)
1 burrata ball, cut in half
crushed pink peppercorns

Make 2 (8-ounce) burger patties, season with salt and pepper, and cook to desired doneness.

Mix the mayo, basil, and balsamic, and spread on the bottom of the bun.

Lay a bed of spring greens on the bottom bun, top with a burger patty, and spoon on a thick layer of bacon tomato jam.

Lay one side of the burrata on top of the jam and sprinkle with peppercorns.

Serves 2

bacon tomato jam

4 pounds heirloom tomatoes, both yellow and red, diced
2 tablespoon kosher salt
6 slices bacon, chopped
1 red onion, chopped
3 cloves garlic, minced
2 tablespoons grated ginger root
3 tablespoons cracked black pepper
1 teaspoon red pepper flakes
½ cup sherry vinegar
1 cup brown sugar

Sprinkle salt over the diced tomatoes, put in a strainer, press down to bruise and push juice out, let sit for an hour, and do another press.

In a large pan, fry the bacon pieces until almost crispy, add the onions and continue to crisp, then add the tomatoes and remaining ingredients.

Bring to a boil, lower heat, simmer until the jam starts to thicken, then chill.

Makes 2 cups

sd grown burger

2 (8-ounce) buffalo burger patties
salt and pepper
2 thick slices of white cheddar
1 tablespoon baconaisse (see recipe, p. 168)
2 brioche buns
coffee-braised onions
2 fried eggs, yolk still runny
microgreens
crushed hemp seed
cheddar popcorn

Season the burger patty with salt and pepper, and cook. Once you flip the burger, lay down a slice of cheese and cook to desired doneness.

Spread the baconaisse on the bottom of the bun, put down the burger with melted cheese, smother in onions, carefully lay the fried egg on top, and garnish with microgreens.

Rub the top of the bun in the pan to coat with fat; this will help the hemp stick to it.

Pat a generous amount of hemp on the bun top. We served it with cheese popcorn.

Serves 2

coffee braised onions

1 1/2 tablespoons butter
1 yellow onion, thickly sliced
1/2 tablespoon rubbed sage
1/2 tablespoon cracked black pepper
1/4 cup double brewed coffee

Melt the butter in a sauté pan and add the onions, sage, and pepper. Continue to cook, slowly adding the coffee and stirring occasionally to prevent charring. Cook until translucent, or until all the liquids have been absorbed.

baconaisse

1 cup mayo
2 slices bacon, cooked until crisp, reserve fat
1 teaspoon garlic powder
½ teaspoon liquid smoke

Blend all the ingredients, including the fat left from cooking the bacon.

Local Help

This burger was designed in collaboration with the following local businesses: Prairie Harvest, Fruit of the Coop, Mary's Kitchen & Gardens, The Source, Dimock Dairy, Dakota Mushroom & Microgreen, Gaylen's Popcorn, Hyatt Family Farm, and Blackshire Farms.

holiday burger

2 (8-ounce) burger patty
sage stuffing spice
2 thick slices of sage derby cheddar
arugula
2 potato buns, toasted
cranberry ketsup
pickled red onions
peppadew peppers

Season the burger patty liberally with sage stuffing spice and cook. Once you flip the burger, lay down the slice of cheese and cook to desired doneness.

Lay a bed of arugula on the bottom of the bun, then place the burger with melted cheese on top.

Spoon a puddle of cranberry ketsup in the center of the burger and top with pickled onions and peppadew.

Serve with sweet potato chips.

Serves 2

sage stuffing spice

2 tablespoons rubbed sage
1 tablespoon thyme leaves
1 tablespoon onion powder
2 tablespoons garlic powder
1 tablespoon crushed black pepper
1 tablespoon celery salt

Combine all ingredients.

cranberry ketsup

2 cups frozen cranberries
2 cups apple juice
¼ cup beef broth
¼ cup balsamic vinegar
2 tablespoons tomato paste
2 tablespoons honey
juice and zest of 1 orange
¼ teaspoon cinnamon
1 teaspoon rubbed sage
1 teaspoon mustard seed
½ teaspoon celery salt

Combine all ingredients in a saucepan and simmer until the cranberries are soft and liquids have reduced.

Cool, then puree.

Makes 2 cups

zinfandelic swiss and mushroom burger

pickled red onions
zinfandel wine, one that is not jammy
½ pound oyster mushrooms, sliced
thyme leaves
garlic powder
2 (8-ounce) wagyu burger patty
2 thick slices gruyère cheese
2 brioche bun, toasted
zinfandel demi-glaze (see recipe below)

Take the pickled red onions from the brine, cover with zinfandel, and let soak for 1 hour.

Sauté the mushrooms in olive oil, sprinkle with thyme and garlic powder, pour a few good splashes of wine into the pan, let reduce, take the mushrooms out of the pan, and hold off to the side.

Put the burger patty in the same pan, cook until almost done, then cover with cheese slices to allow melting.

Place the burger on the toasted bottom bun, top with mushrooms, drizzle with some of the demi-glace, and garnish with pickled zinfandel onions.

Serve with extra demi-glace on the side to smother at will and BBQ potato chips.

Serves 2

zinfandel demi-glaze

¼ cup butter
2 tablespoons minced garlic
1 tablespoons cracked black pepper
1 cup zinfandel
1 cup beef stock

In a saucepan, melt the butter, add the garlic to lightly brown, whisk in the remaining ingredients, and bring to a boil. Reduce heat and simmer until reduced by half.

elke sommer burger

2 (8-ounce) colorado ground elk patty
beer-braised onions (see recipe, p. 172)
2 thick slices of butterkäse cheese
2 potato bun, toasted
sauerkraut
pickle relish
düsseldorf mustard

Cook your elk patty in a sauté pan. Once you turn it to cook the other side, put a heaping spoonful of the onions on top, and when almost done, put on the slice of cheese to melt.

On the bottom of the toasted bun, lay a bed of sauerkraut, top with the burger, spoon on relish, spread mustard on the top bun, and serve with pretzels and pickles.

Serves 2

Elke Origins

This burger was a tribute to a German classic! Elke Sommer was an actress and pin up girl in the sixties and seventies, known for her sky-high bouffant hairdo and deep, husky voice.

beer lover's burger

2 (8-ounce) burger patty
2 pretzel bun, toasted
sauerkraut
beer cheese sauce
beer-braised onions

Season and cook the burger to your preference of doneness.

On the bottom of the pretzel bun, lay a bed of sauerkraut, top with the burger patty, ladle on the beer cheese sauce, and top with beer-braised onions.

Serve with Guinness chips and a snit of beer. We used our local Fernson Lion's Paw Lager.

Serves 2

beer cheese sauce

4 tablespoons butter
4 tablespoons flour
6 ounces lager beer
1 cup heavy cream
1 teaspoon whole grain mustard
1 teaspoon worcestershire sauce
1 teaspoon nutmeg
½ teaspoon garlic salt
¼ teaspoon white pepper
2 cups shredded mild cheddar
8 ounces brick cheese, thinly sliced

In a saucepan, melt the butter, slowly add the flour, whisking until creamy, and cook for a couple of minutes.

Gradually add the beer and cream, whisking continuously.

Stir in the mustard, worcestershire sauce, and spices.

Add the cheese, stirring until melted. Allow to cook on low until thickened.

Makes 3 – 4 cups

beer-braised onions

3 tablespoons butter
3 yellow onions, thickly sliced
1 tablespoon thyme leaves
8 ounces lager beer

Melt the butter in a sauté pan, then add the onions and thyme. Cook until translucent, then slowly add the beer, continuing to cook, stirring occasionally to prevent charring. As soon as the liquids have been absorbed, the onions are done.

guacAmole burger

2 (8-ounce) lamb burger patty
2 brioche bun, toasted
mole sauce (see recipe below)
cotija cheese, crumbled
radish, thinly sliced for garnish
radish microgreens for garnish
guacamole
peppadew pepper for garnish

Season and cook the burger to your preference, then lay it on the bottom bun, top with dollops of mole sauce, and sprinkle with cheese.

Garnish with microgreens and radish slices.

Spread guacamole on the top bun and garnish with a peppadew pepper.

Serve with tortilla chips.

Serves 2

mole sauce

1 ounce each of these 3 peppers: dried ancho, chipotle, and de árbol chilis
½ tablespoon sesame seeds
1 tablespoon coriander seeds
3 tablespoons pepitas
3 tablespoons peanuts
2 tablespoons olive oil
1 small white onion, chopped
2 tablespoons raisins
½ teaspoon cinnamon
¼ teaspoon cloves
1 teaspoon chili powder
½ teaspoon mexican oregano
4 corn chips
2 tablespoons tomato paste
2 cups beef broth
1 teaspoon honey
3 tablespoons finely chopped dark chocolate
salt to taste

Place the peppers in a bowl, cover them with boiling water, let them sit for about 30 minutes, drain, remove the stems and seeds, and mince.

While the peppers are soaking, toast the sesame seeds, coriander seeds, pepitas, and peanuts in a skillet, just until fragrant. Add the olive oil and onions to the pan and sauté until the onions are translucent.

Put the sauteed onion mixture in a food processor, along with the peppers, raisins, cinnamon, cloves, chili powder, oregano, corn chips, tomato paste and 1 cup of the broth.

Process until it turns into a creamy paste, adding more broth if necessary, to keep it smooth.

Put the paste in a saucepan and cook, stirring constantly while adding the rest of the broth and the honey. Simmer on low until thick and shiny, but it should be a little thinner than you want it to be. Then fold in the chocolate and cook a few minutes longer. Salt to taste.

Makes approximately 1 pint

guacamole

3 ripe avocados, pitted and scooped out
1 roma tomato, minced
1 green onion, minced
1 tablespoon minced jalapeño
1 teaspoon lime juice
2 tablespoons mayonnaise
1 tablespoon finely minced cilantro
½ teaspoon sea salt

Combine all ingredients in a bowl and mix thoroughly with a fork. If you want it creamy, put it in a food processor to blend.

Serves 4

You can tell we put a lot of thought into our burgers. The last recipe here, created in tribute to National "Save the Bee" Week, shows the amount of research that was put into all our menu items. Despite my allergy to bees, curiosity brought me out to the country, to where we bought our honey, Cradle to Grave Farms.

honeybee burger

spicy honey butter (see recipe below)
2 brioche bun, toasted
2 (8-ounce) burger patty, seasoned and cooked to your preference
4 ounces honey goat gouda, shredded
honeycomb, cut two ¾-inch squares
spring mix greens
pickled jalapeños and edible wildflowers for garnish

Spread honey butter on the bottom bun, lay down a bed of greens, put down the burger, top with cheese, place the honeycomb on top, and garnish with jalapeño slices and edible wildflowers.

Serve with honey BBQ chips and enjoy with a glass of Wild Man honey hopped mead!

Serves 2

spicy honey butter

½ cup butter, softened to room temperature
2 tablespoons honey
1 tablespoon green chili hot sauce
1 tablespoon minced fresh rosemary

Blend all ingredients thoroughly.

Before giving in to placing a burger on the menu, I tried to appease the ground meat cravings of our customers with meatballs. They vary from the size of a pea to an orange, made from poultry, fish, or meat. With almost every country having their own version, we could come up with as many versions as we did our burgers. Our theme of wine bar cuisine certainly suited the Italian and Swedish meatballs.

italian meatball skillet

1 fennel bulb, sliced, save some fronds for garnish
1 yellow onion, sliced
1 green bell pepper, sliced
1 red bell pepper, sliced
1 tablespoon fennel seed
1 cup marinara sauce*
¼ cup chopped fresh basil leaves*
12 italian meatballs (see recipe, p. 178)
4 thick slices provolone
italian seasoning for garnish

*You can use marinara and add basil, but we used our tomato basil chianti soup reduced down to sauce consistency, delicious!

Sauté the vegetable slices and fennel seed in olive oil until the onions are translucent. Add the marinara sauce and meatballs. Cook until just warmed.

Spoon the vegetables and sauce into 4 mini cast iron skillets. Place 3 meatballs on top of each. Cover with provolone cheese.

Place the skillets on a large baking sheet. Cook at 400 degrees until the sauce is bubbling and the cheese is browned, about 15 minutes.

Garnish the top with fennel fronds and sprinkled italian seasoning. Serve with a toasted baguette.

Serves 4

italian meatballs

½ cup panko bread crumbs
6 tablespoons milk
2 pounds ground beef
½ pound ground pork
2 tablespoons minced garlic
1 yellow onion, finely minced
¼ cup grated parmigiano reggiano
2 tablespoons worcestershire sauce
1 tablespoon nutmeg
2 teaspoons thyme
2 teaspoons italian seasoning
2 teaspoons red pepper flakes
1 teaspoon black pepper
1 teaspoon dry mustard
¼ cup finely chopped parsley
2 teaspoons salt
2 large eggs

Soak the panko in the milk. Add to all the remaining ingredients. Mix with your hands until just blended; overworking the meat will result in a tough meatball. Roll into equal-sized balls weighing about 3 ounces each. Lay them on a paper-lined baking sheet and cook at 350 degrees for 15–20 minutes. You can freeze the extra meatballs for later use as an appetizer or with spaghetti.

Makes approximately 12 – 16 meatballs

swedish meatballs in gravy

½ cup butter
½ cup flour
½ teaspoon nutmeg
4 cups beef broth
3 tablespoons worcestershire sauce
1 tablespoon dijon mustard
salt and pepper

1 cup sour cream
16 swedish meatballs (see recipe p. 179)
4 pappardelle pasta nests
½ cup lingonberries
pickled red onion, minced green onion, and rosemary for garnish

Melt the butter in a large saucepan, then add the flour and nutmeg, stirring until it forms a creamy paste. Gradually add the beef broth, worcestershire sauce, and mustard. Cook over medium heat until thickened. Season with salt and pepper to taste. Stir in the sour cream.

Add the cooked meatballs to the warm sauce.

Cook the 4 pappardelle pasta nests al dente, and drain well, do not rinse.

Lay a nest of pasta in each of 4 dishes. Place 4 meatballs on top of each and cover with sauce. Top with a spoonful of lingonberries. Garnish with pickled red onion, minced green onion, and rosemary.

Serves 4

swedish meatballs

- 1/3 cup panko breadcrumbs
- 5 tablespoons milk
- 1 ¼ pounds ground beef
- ¾ pounds ground pork
- 1 ¼ tablespoons minced garlic
- 1 small yellow onion, finely minced
- 1/3 cup finely grated swiss cheese
- 1 ¼ tablespoons worcestershire sauce
- 2 tablespoons nutmeg
- 1/3 teaspoon allspice
- 1 ¼ teaspoon thyme
- 1 ¼ teaspoon white pepper
- 1 ¼ teaspoon dry mustard
- 2 ½ tablespoons finely chopped parsley
- 1 ¼ teaspoon salt
- 2 large eggs

Soak the panko in milk. Add to all the remaining ingredients. Mix with your hands until just blended; overworking the meat will result in a tough meatball. Roll into equal-sized balls. Lay them on a paper-lined baking sheet and cook at 350 degrees for 15 minutes.

Makes approximately 16 meatballs

Lingonberries

Lingonberries are embraced by the Scandinavian countries. They're a smaller cousin to the cranberry, similar in flavor but juicier. Traditionally used on meatballs, pancakes, and rice pudding, they are now being seen used in wild game and poultry dishes.

guys and gals in the kitchen...

Having a small menu is beneficial not only for the freshness of ingredients, or satisfying seasonal appetites and cravings, it also allows for creativity and a challenge for the team. Basically, there are two types of kitchens, one that offers the same items every day and one like ours that changes almost daily. Some cooks thrive on routine, knowing exactly what they must do on a daily basis, and they do it well. Then you have chefs that grow bored with repetition and need that extra stimulation. I have shared my kitchen with both kinds throughout the years.

Employees come and go; it is the nature of the beast. But in the kitchen I was blessed with two people who, for different reasons, were particularly special to me, Sam Allen and Greg Springer. They thrived on challenges and learning new things. You often hear about the reputation of arrogant chefs that can be difficult to work with. This was not true of them.

Sam began with us from the very start of The Market. He was our youngest, still a high school student. When we were moving from the other location, Sam was on a school trip to Germany, so he had his brother, Seth, stand in for him and help us out. This was the start to a wonderful working relationship.

It was hard to believe that this was Sam's first job. Starting as a dishwasher, he quickly worked his way into prep and line duties. Sam grew up watching the Food Channel and had a passionate desire to learn as much as he could. He and Greg were a good team, feeding off each other's curiosity. With a love for knives, Sam was a ninja in our kitchen full of charcuterie. It was a pleasure watching his skills and social prowess grow through the years.

As much as he loved knives, Sam really adored bacon. When the weather was nice, we would make ourselves something to eat and enjoy the fresh air out on the patio. One day Sam came out to join us with his newest creation, a bacon grilled cheese sandwich wrapped in bacon!! We all had a big chuckle, but it was delicious.

sam's ultimate bacon grilled cheese sandwich

2 slices sourdough bread
4 slices fresh mozzarella
1 thick slice provolone
bacon jam (see recipe, p. 193)
6 slices bacon

Make a sandwich with the bread, cheeses, and a thick layer of bacon jam.

Lay out 3 strips of bacon next to each other, lay the sandwich on one end of the strips, and bring the ends up to wrap it.

Lay down another 3 strips of bacon perpendicular to the other strips and wrap again.

Sear both sides in a skillet until crispy, 5–7 minutes per side, draining any excess bacon fat.

Sam had a natural talent that was refreshing to work with. Greg, on the other hand, had studied at Le Cordon Bleu College of Culinary Arts in Minneapolis. He had a unique style of good down-home cooking finished with a technical finesse. A champion on the line, no matter how busy it got, he maintained a calmness and put out clean plates in a timely manner.

Every chef has a particular area of comfort. For example, I love to make soup, sauces, and one-pan dishes, such as sauté and casserole. The blending of flavors excites me. Greg had a natural affinity for meat preparations. He meticulously worked with the different cuts to bring out the best of their attributes. If you heard country music blaring from the kitchen, most likely you would find him butchering a pig, rubbing a pork belly, or making sausage.

Our visit to the Witt's End Farm, where we purchased our pigs, helped us to understand what they were fed and how they were housed. The tenderness and flavor of the meat comes not only from the breed itself but also from its environment. Greg used this knowledge to appreciate the quality of the meat and how he would use it. No parts went to waste; his creativity grew with each subsequent pig.

I believed that Chef Greg's finest treatment was that of the pork belly. He made pancetta, cured, and smoked bacon, but his low and slow-roasted, caramelized belly was sublime. Much like the loin, the taste of the belly meat itself is mild. The flavor all comes from the fat. While baking, the fat breaks down, pulling in the essence of the rub.

pork belly with pork caramel and spring veggies

1½ pounds fingerling potatoes
2 pounds pork belly, cured and precooked
2 tablespoons butter
4 cups fresh morel mushrooms or 2 ounces dried and rehydrated
24 ramps
salt and pepper
pork caramel sauce (see recipe below)

Rub the potatoes with olive oil, put on a baking sheet, and sprinkle with sea salt crystals.

Place the pork belly pieces, cut in 1½-inch squares, on the same tray, skin-side-up. Cook at 350 degrees until the potatoes are fork tender, about 24 minutes.

About five minutes before the potatoes and pork are done, melt the butter in a sauté pan on high heat. Add the morels and ramps; do not overcook, you are basically just warming. Add salt and pepper to taste.

Assemble 4 plates: Place potatoes in the middle of the plate and top with ramps. Place mushrooms around them. Layer with pork belly, then generously drizzle with warm pork caramel sauce.

Serves 4

pork caramel sauce

½ cup brown sugar
4 tablespoons water (if you used dried morels, use the dehydration water)
4 tablespoons sherry vinegar
2 cups pork broth
1 teaspoon butter

Dissolve the sugar and water in a saucepan and bring to a boil. Gently boil until it is slightly thickening. Stir in the vinegar and broth. Continue to cook at a simmer until it reduces and thickens. Remove from heat. Fold in butter.

beet caprese with juniper pork belly

1 golden beet
1 red beet
¼ cup juniper berries (can substitute fresh cranberries)
¼ cup pinot noir
1 tablespoon honey
¼ cup orange juice
¼ cup olive oil
6 fresh basil leaves
½-pound pork belly (pre-cured and cooked)
1 tablespoon orange marmalade
1 (8-ounce) fresh mozzarella ball, thick sliced
2 tablespoons balsamic glaze
arugula microgreens for garnish
basil oil

Wrap the beets individually with foil. Roast them in a 400-degree oven until tender, about 1 hour. When cool enough to handle, peel and cut into thick slices.

While the beets are cooking, put the berries in a small saucepan with the pinot noir, honey, and orange juice. Simmer until the berries are plump and have absorbed the liquid.

Blend the olive oil and basil leaves on high speed.

When the beets have cooked for half an hour, cut the pork belly in squares to fit appropriately to the size of the beets, then put the pork belly in the oven to warm it up and crisp the skin. When you take it out, spoon the marmalade and some of the juniper berries over the top of the pork to act as a glaze.

Alternate layers of beets and mozzarella in a stack. Drizzle with basil oil and balsamic glaze.

With a long skewer, attach the pork belly to the top of the beet stack.

Drain any excess liquid from the berries and scatter them about the plate. Garnish with microgreens.

Serves 2

When you cook from scratch, there is a lot of prep. Finding someone that has good knife skills and takes instructions well can be hard. We got lucky when Sharon Hoover joined the team. She is one of the sweetest and hardest working people in the local restaurant scene, usually holding down two to three jobs at a time. As soon as she got there, the guys could take their break and know that when they came back, the soup and salad area would be prepped and ready for the night.

I was very meticulous about plate presentation, much to the chagrin of some employees. But Sharon tried hard to match my expectations. Photos saved on her cell phone became her study guides. When I asked Sharon what was one of the plates she was most proud of, she sent me a picture of a salad that had evolved throughout a terribly busy June week, yet she'd proudly nailed it every time. It began as a summer solstice salad, then salad juliana, both with cucumber curls that she meticulously worked with. The third salad of the week, orange salmon salad, was so popular that it found its way onto the regular menu.

yuzu orange salmon salad

4 tablespoons butter
1 yellow onion, thinly sliced
1 fennel bulb, thinly sliced
¼ cup orange juice
1 tablespoon minced orange rind
2 (6-ounce) verlasso salmon filet
mixed greens
24 fresh mint leaves
yuzu-kosho dressing
8 fennel fronds
crushed pink peppercorns
2 navel orange, peeled, sliced
¼-inch thick
microgreens for garnish
2 edible orchids

Melt the butter in a sauté pan, add the onion and fennel, and once the onions are translucent and the fennel has softened, add the orange juice and orange rind, and allow to reduce into a glaze.

Meanwhile, pan fry the salmon, seasoned to your liking.

Mix the greens and mint leaves lightly in the dressing and place in the middle of a serving dish.

Tuck the fennel fronds on the outside of the salad.

Place the salmon filet on top of the greens, sprinkle with crushed pink peppercorns, fan a layer of orange slices on top of salmon, finish with a large dollop of the onion/fennel mix, garnish with microgreens.

Tear petals from the orchid and sprinkle on the plate.

Serves 2

yuzu-kosho dressing

1 tablespoon yuzu marmalade
1 teaspoon minced jalapeño
1 teaspoon soy sauce
2 tablespoons rice vinegar
¼ cup olive oil

Blend the ingredients well.

Kewpie

Kewpie, the best brand of Japanese mayo, has always been used and sold in The Market. Then they came out with their yuzu-kosho dressing. Yuzu is a citrus fruit that is known for its highly aromatic rind that keeps its sourness even after cooking. Not only is it wonderful for dressing but also for marinades!

halibut summer solstice salad

2 cups mixed greens
12 fresh mint leaves
12 fresh basil leaves
yuzu-kosho dressing (see recipe, p. 187)
1 tablespoon fresh chives, minced, save a blossom head for garnish
2 cucumbers, cut in thin, long ribbons
pea shoots
1 watermelon radish, sliced into thin half moons
2 tablespoons fresh dill weed
16 asparagus spears, roasted
1 large rhubarb stalk, cut in 1 inch pieces, roasted
2 (4 ounce) halibut filets

Toss the mixed greens, mint leaves, and basil leaves with a light coating of dressing, then sprinkle chives on top.

Wind in the cucumber slices, tucking some pea shoots into one curl, then laying another pinch on the side.

On the outside of the greens, tuck in the radish slices, dill weed, and 2 bundles of asparagus.

Pan-sear or grill the halibut. Place on top of the salad, between cucumber curls, brush lightly with dressing, top with rhubarb, and garnish with chive blossom.

Serves 2

We utilized many of the same ingredients for another version of that salad. Our neighbor in the Harvester Building was a lovely women's shop, Juliana's Boutique la Femme, owned by Julie Haagenson and Lana Olshove. Our shared friendship and business relationship led to many joint adventures. We had a lot of fun during the "planning meetings," but they always ended with the perfect event in-the-making.

The weather we were having that week was delightful. What perfect timing to host a ladies' luncheon and fashion show out on the patio. The girls and I would be the models for a fun change of pace. So, while the women in the audience enjoyed some bubbly and this salad, we strutted our stuff.

salad juliana: roasted rhubarb and herb salad

2 cups mixed greens
16 fresh mint leaves
12 fresh basil leaves
ginger herb vinaigrette
(see recipe, p. 190)
1 green onion, sliced
½ cup fresh peas, lightly steamed
pea sprouts
1 watermelon radish, sliced into thin half moons
12 asparagus spears, roasted
12 cup rhubarb pieces, roasted
chive blossom head for garnish

Lightly toss the greens, mint, and basil with the vinaigrette.

Place the salad in the middle of a plate, top with a handful of peas and green onions.

Cut a bundle of pea sprouts so they have a flat bottom, and stand them up in the greens.

Tuck the radish slices and asparagus into the outside of the salad.

Top with the rhubarb and the chive blossom.

I served this salad with a strawberry muffin.

Serves 2

ginger herb vinaigrette

¾ cup extra virgin olive oil
¼ cup strawberry vinegar
2 tablespoons rice vinegar
1 teaspoon crushed fennel seed
1 minced garlic clove
2 tablespoons grated ginger root
1 teaspoon honey
2 tablespoons minced fresh parsley
2 tablespoons minced fresh dill
¼ teaspoon salt

Mix all the ingredients in a blender.

Makes 1 cup

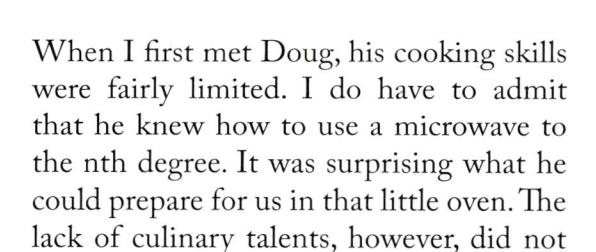

When I first met Doug, his cooking skills were fairly limited. I do have to admit that he knew how to use a microwave to the nth degree. It was surprising what he could prepare for us in that little oven. The lack of culinary talents, however, did not diminish his good taste in food.

We enjoyed dining out when traveling, always on a quest for something new. When we cooked at home, Doug was taking it all in, his enthusiasm for nouvelle cuisine mounting. As with many men, grilling and smoking were a focus of interest. Since he'd had the nickname of "Torchie" as a kid, this only makes sense.

When Mike gave Bertha the Grill to The Market, it was an exciting day for Doug and Greg. Previously, we'd had a small grill and separate smoking unit that they tediously cooked small batches on. Bertha not only made life easier for them, but also allowed for a newfound creativity.

There is something euphoric about the aroma that fills the air when you're smoking pork. The dripping juices hit the hot charcoal and applewood, creating a cloud that lures customers in for blocks around. From the first day we opened, there was always pulled pork on the menu. Except for the turkey sandwich that we brought back from the Food n' Fermentations days, the pork was the favorite on the menu.

Sometimes it was a traditional pulled pork with BBQ sauce, but more often than not, we offered unique versions. The three little pigs and the italian pork were the two most popular. The success of these sandwiches couldn't have happened without a perfectly cooked pork shoulder. The recipe is called pos's pulled pork in honor of Mike, who taught us how to make it on Bertha. Pos is a longtime nickname shortened from his last name of Pospischil.

pos's pulled pork

½ cup brown sugar
¼ cup kosher salt
¼ cup cracked black pepper
1 teaspoon paprika
2 teaspoons garlic powder
1 (4-pound) pork shoulder, bone-in
4 cups pork broth
2 tablespoons caraway seed
2 tablespoons minced garlic
2 tablespoons worcestershire sauce
1 tablespoon liquid smoke

Make the rub: Thoroughly blend the sugar, salt, pepper, paprika, and garlic powder. Massage this mixture on all sides of the pork roast, pressing it into the meat. Cover and refrigerate overnight.

Cook the pork: Put the meat in a smoker, using half charcoal, half applewood. Cook for 4 hours at 175 degrees. Take it out of the smoker and put it in a roasting pan. Add the pork broth, caraway, garlic, worcestershire, and liquid smoke. Cover and cook at 300 degrees for 4 more hours. The meat will separate easily, and the bone pull right out. Pull the meat apart with claws or gloved hands. Leave in the pan juices.

Makes approximately 2 pounds or more of cooked meat.

The three little pigs sandwich went through a couple of different versions. Originally it started out with pulled pork, corn cob smoked ham, and bacon jam on a croissant bun. Then, using the same ingredients, we changed it to an open-faced presentation on sourdough bread and topped it with an egg. The last transformation was renamed the three pigs and a duck, switching the ham for lardo and using a duck egg.

three pigs and a duck

2 thick slices of sourdough bread
¼ cup whipped lardo (see recipe below)
1 cup pulled pork
¼ cup bacon jam
2 duck eggs, fried
1 tablespoon sap sago cheese, grated, for garnish
crushed pink peppercorns for garnish

Brush one side of a slice of the bread with olive oil and grill to golden brown. Spread a thick layer of lardo on the grilled side of the bread. Top with hot pulled pork, then spread with bacon jam. Top with the fried duck egg, yolk still runny. Garnish with grated cheese and pink peppercorns.

Serves 2

whipped lardo

1 pound pork back fat
3 roasted garlic cloves, smashed
1 teaspoon sea salt
1 tablespoon crushed pink peppercorns
2 tablespoons finely chopped fresh rosemary
2 teaspoons sherry vinegar

Run the pork fat through a fine grind. Put it in a mixing bowl and add the spices and sherry vinegar. Blend with a paddle, starting on low speed and gradually working up to high speed. Let it run for at least 5 minutes, until light and airy.

Makes 1 cup

bacon jam

3 pounds bacon, diced
2 yellow onions, finely chopped
2 teaspoons minced garlic
½ cup lemon juice
1 cup apple cider vinegar
1 cup brown sugar
1 cup maple syrup
2 teaspoons dijon mustard
2 teaspoons worcestershire sauce
2 cups coffee
½ teaspoons cayenne pepper

In a large saucepan, cook the bacon until almost crispy. Add the onion and cook, stirring often, until the onions are caramelized, about 15 minutes.

Stir in the remaining ingredients. Bring the mixture to a simmer, then reduce heat to low. Cook until the liquid has reduced and thickened, but is not quite jammy. This takes a few hours, so be patient and stir often. There will be a layer of bacon fat on top; do not skim it off.

Refrigerate overnight. When ready to use, stir in the fat layer.

Makes approximately 1 quart

italian pulled pork

12 ounces pulled pork
2 cup pork broth
1 yellow onion
1 red bell pepper
1 large baguette
4 slices provolone cheese
dried oregano
dried thyme
fresh rosemary
crushed fennel seed
¼ cup tomato juice

Heat the pulled pork in the pork broth.

Slice the onions and peppers, and sauté in olive oil until the onions are translucent.

Cut the ends off the baguette, then cut in half and slice open. Brush with olive oil and toast.

Remove the pork from the pan, saving the broth. On a griddle or in a sauté pan, portion the pork into a sandwich-sized pile, layer with the sauteed peppers and onions, and top with cheese. Cover to allow the steam to melt the cheese. Carefully use a spatula to place on the bottom of the baguette.

Liberally sprinkle with the oregano, thyme, rosemary, and fennel.

Mix the hot pork broth with tomato juice in a ramekin for dipping.

Serves 2

I am a lover of all foods—well, not lutefisk or fried bologna, so, most foods. Always willing to try something new and explore different cultural diets, I was curious about our cooks Ben and Chris's vegan lifestyles. Watching as they prepared their own lunches, I usually was not too tempted, but I must admit, a couple of dishes were very enticing.

They had to cook meat on a day-to-day basis and did so without preaching about their dietary beliefs. In appreciation for this, we started to host Vegan Tuesday to allow for their culinary expression. With the growing demand and popularity of veganism, we eventually added a few dishes to our menu.

I loved Chris's chickpea of the sea; it was so fresh and bright, yet filling. When he was making it, you had to keep me away with my tasting spoons; I could eat the entire bowl before it ever made it to the plate!

chris's chickpea of the sea

1 red bell pepper
1 red onion
1 jalapeño pepper, de-seeded
12 ounces dill pickles
6 cups cooked garbanzo beans
3 tablespoons stone-ground mustard
¾ cup veganaise
2 tablespoons pickle juice
1 tablespoon dill weed
salt and pepper to taste
8 slices egg-free artisan bread
arugula
2 tomatoes, sliced
½ cup maple smoked cashews

Finely dice the red pepper, red onion, jalapeño, and pickles.

Roughly mash the garbanzo beans, leaving some chunks for texture.

Fold in the diced veggies, mustard, veganaise, pickle juice, and dill weed.

Season to taste with salt and pepper.

Thickly slice the bread, brush one side with olive oil, and lightly grill. Top with a layer of arugula and tomato slices. Spoon on a cup of the filling. Garnish with cashews.

Serves 8

Since we were known for our pulled pork sandwiches and macNcheese, Ben and Chris's vegan versions were a perfect fit. It was also a great way to showcase the fresh local oyster mushrooms we had available.

vegan "pulled pork" sandwich

1 pound oyster mushrooms
1 dozen canned artichoke heart quarters
olive oil
vegan BBQ sauce
4 banh mi buns, grilled
arugula
pickle slices for garnish

Shred the mushrooms with a fork or slice thinly into strips, then chop the artichoke quarters.

Heat the olive oil and lightly sauté the mushrooms and artichokes, until warm.

Toss lightly with the BBQ sauce.

On the bun, lay a bed of arugula, top with the mushroom mixture, and garnish with pickle slices.

Serves 4

vegan mac & cheese

1½ cups raw cashews
½ cup water
½ cup coconut milk
1 tablespoon miso paste
2 tablespoons lemon juice
½ cup nutritional yeast
½ teaspoon garlic powder
½ teaspoon onion powder
¼ teaspoon turmeric
⅛ teaspoon nutmeg
1 (12-ounce) package egg-free macaroni, cooked al dente
salt and pepper to taste

Cover the cashews with boiling water and allow to soak for 2–4 hours, then drain.

Mix the water, coconut milk, miso, lemon juice, yeast, and spices in a food processor until smooth.

Transfer to a pot, stir while heating, and fold in the cooked pasta.

Serves 4 - 6

Dakota Mushroom and Microgreens

Dan is the proprietor of Dakota Mushroom and Microgreens. He has brought joy to restaurateurs and farmers market shoppers with his variety of produce grown in an innovative warehouse right here in Sioux Falls. The quality of the mushrooms and the variety of microgreens were stars in many of our dishes.

specialties to be proud of...

Salmon was another delicacy that Bertha infused with flavor. We used two different Atlantic varieties with regularity, Verlasso and Faroe Island. Verlasso was most commonly available, shipped fresh twice a week. It is harvested from the glacier inlets of Patagonia, Chile. The Capera Island farm is one of the most sustainable in the world. The deep, cold waters and the large space that they allow the fish to swim in are just two of the reasons Verlasso is superior to other farmed salmon. Conventionally farmed salmon usually has a fat level of 18 percent, whereas Verlasso is only 11 percent, contributing to its milder flavor, clean, not fishy smell, and firm, flaky meat.

The same can be said about the farms of Denmark's Faroe Island. The remote location is already a natural feeding ground for wild Atlantic salmon leaving the rivers of Europe to grow before heading back to spawn. This salmon has a buttery taste, with a little more marbling than Verlasso. The extra fat content makes it perfect for grilling.

Late one summer, we hosted one of our "Picnic with a Winemaker" events with King Estate Winery from Eugene, Oregon. Because they are famous for their pinot noir and pinot gris, we knew salmon was going to be the perfect option to serve with their wine. Oregon is also known for microbreweries, so our thought was to elevate the flavor by smoking the salmon with hops.

The folks from Cradle to Grave Farms, a local grower of hops, barley, and grapes, gladly worked with us on this endeavor. After trial and error, we learned that the trick to success was to use fresh cut vines soaked in water immediately, leaving them in the water until ready to put on the grill. Equally important was using a low heat to avoid flare-ups.

Before the dinner began, the guys gathered around Bertha, curious about the unique aroma. The fresh Faroe Island salmon that had arrived earlier in the day were now beautiful coral filets cradled in a smoky hop nest. The bitter, citrusy flavor that was infused into the fatty meat was delectable.

hop-smoked salmon

Cut enough hops to have a full nest of vines for your filet and fully submerge them in a bucket of water.

Using tweezers, take out the pin bones that run along the top of the fillet and off the spine.

Trim off the belly following the natural contours of the fish. Save the belly for other preparations.

Rinse under cold water and pat dry, then season. Since we used high-quality salmon, we only used sea salt and cracked pepper. If you want to rub with seasoning such as cajun or herbs, do so now.

Bring your smoker to 225 degrees; we used a mixture of charcoal and apple wood.

Place the hop vines on the rack and nestle your filets, skin-down, into it.

Cook until the salmon reaches 140 degrees, do not overcook!

Let sit for 10 minutes before cutting into it.

Good, fresh seafood is such a rarity around here. Apart from chain restaurants offering shrimp and lobster, it's pretty much slim pickings. True seafood lovers got lucky when SurfsUp opened downtown. Mike and Barb were bringing in unique items not yet seen in Sioux Falls. It was a dining experience that was greatly missed when they closed.

Wanting to keep that spark alive, we began a monthly SurfsUp Saturday dinner. Mike introduced me to the fishmongers he had been dealing with. This opened a whole new side of the culinary industry to me. It was exciting to learn about the fishing zones and seasons. Knowing where our food was coming from was important to me, and this started a whole new set of discoveries.

From geoduck to octopus, blowfish to halibut, we tried it all. Opening the boxes when they arrived was always exciting. Our delivery man was particularly intrigued the day we received two exceedingly long boxes from California. Inside each was a freshly caught, whole mako shark from the Pacific Coast.

The guys got to work right away, rubbing the inside cavity with spices, stuffing it full of fruit, vegetables, and herbs. They had to be careful not to scratch their arms against the skin like sandpaper. After being wrapped in banana leaves, the sharks were put in Bertha to slowly cook.

The patio was full of guests waiting in anticipation for the official unveiling. The aroma released when Chef Greg opened the lid filled the air with sweet, smoky pineapple. He cut open the banana leaves, revealing thick, firm meat that was like swordfish but moister, with a sweet, not so wild taste. Everyone was pleasantly surprised just how delicious it was. It was worth the wait and all the work.

The most popular of all SurfsUp nights was the seafood boil. The enthusiasm for the day ran high among the cabana-shirted staff and customers. It took hours to prep all the ingredients and fill the mesh bags. Once the final package was knotted, the fun began. Mike would come down and help Greg man the steam pots. It was a hot job, but I made sure to keep the guys hydrated with cold grain belts and chardonnay. Luckily, the sound of cracking crab shells and laughter drowned out the bad jokes being shared over the pots!

seafood boil for two

1 lemon, cut in half
1 large yellow onion, chopped
4 cloves garlic
4 tablespoons melted butter
1 teaspoon Tabasco sauce
½ cup sauvignon blanc
¼ cup Old Bay seasoning
¼ cup pickling spice
10 ounces cod
8 green lip mussels

6 colossal shrimp (U/10), shell on
20 ounces snow crab legs (2 clusters)
4 fresh cherrystone clams
2 (4-ounce) andouille sausage links, cut in half
1 corn cob, cut in half
16 small baby red potatoes, with holes poked into them with a fork
1 yellow onion, cut in half

Fill a large stockpot with enough water to cover your seafood packages.

Add the lemon, chopped onions, garlic, butter, Tabasco, wine, and seasonings, bring to boil, and let simmer while you make your boiling package.

Stuff the seafood, sausage, corn, potatoes, and onion, equal portions, into 2 mesh boiling bags. Drop into the seasoned boiling water and cook for 8–10 minutes.

Serve on a tray with lots of melted butter and napkins.

Serves 2

In my younger years, my dad, who was in the Air Force, was stationed in Anchorage, Alaska. It was the land of earthquakes, moose hunting, huge cabbage, and crabbing. I remember the guys putting halibut heads in the net, throwing them over the dock, and waiting. The net would shake as the crab went after the bait. Once it was pulled up there would be enough kings to fill a duffel bag. We lived on crab meat, sockeye salmon from the Kenai River, and halibut. If only I could enjoy that diet now.

herbed halibut and veggie packet

6 spears asparagus
½ zucchini, sliced
¼ cup corn
¼ yellow onion, sliced
¼ red bell pepper, chopped
salt and pepper
4 ounces halibut
dill weed
2 tablespoons butter
4 chopped fresh basil leaves
sprigs of fresh thyme
sprigs of fresh tarragon
4 lemon slices
2 tablespoons white wine, I prefer sauvignon blanc

Lay down a sheet of foil, layer the vegetables in the middle of the sheet, and sprinkle with salt and pepper.

Place the fish on top, sprinkle with dill weed, dot with butter, and cover with fresh herbs and lemon.

Bring up the edges of the foil, add the wine, and fold up and seal the edges so steam doesn't escape.

Place the packet on a baking sheet in case of a leak.

Bake at 400 degrees for about 12 minutes, or on the grill for about 10 minutes, depending on the thickness of the fish.

To serve, cut open the packet and enjoy directly from there, or carefully slide the contents onto a plate, including the juices.

halibut in harissa broth

2 cups seafood broth
4 cups vegetable broth
1 tablespoon onion powder
1 tablespoon minced garlic
1 (2-inch) piece ginger root, thinly sliced
3 tablespoons harissa paste
1 cup non-oaked chardonnay
2 fennel bulbs, cut into wedges
1 preserved meyer lemon, sliced
4 (6-ounce) halibut filets
1 pound asparagus spears
1 cup mixed olives, pitted, cut in half
¼ cup black olive tapenade

In a sauce pot, combine the broth, onion powder, garlic, ginger, and harissa, simmer until a ¼ of the broth is reduced. Pour in the wine and return to a low simmer for another 15 minutes.

Add the fennel and meyer lemon, and cook until tender, about 10 minutes, then turn down heat and keep warm over medium-low heat.

Meanwhile, sauté the halibut in olive oil, cooking for 3–4 minutes.

Flip the fillets and cook until the fish is starting to flake, about 3 minutes more.

Once you flip the fish, add the asparagus and olives to the broth and turn up heat.

To serve, place the fish in the middle of a serving dish and arrange the fennel, olives, and asparagus around it. Ladle hot broth over top. Garnish with olive tapenade.

Serves 4

Halibut

When halibut are hatched, they look like any other fish and swim upright. After six months, however, their bodies begin to flatten out and one eye shifts to the other side. The halibut then begins to swim flat along the ocean floor eating small fish, squid, and crustaceans.

Even before we started the SurfsUp evenings, seafood was held in high esteem at The Market. Beginning back at The Market on Phillips, we held a New Year's Eve celebration of champagne and caviar. We were the place to go to start your New Year's festivities in style. At high noon, the corks started flying and pearls of caviar were popping!

After the first year, I started making my lobster bisque to give everyone something a little more substantial yet luxurious. For the months following, people would beg me to make another batch, but I always held my ground and only made it to be treasured on this special day.

This tradition has continued, with caviar and champagne in abundance, bowls of bisque at every table, and great memories shared from the year soon to be past. It's easy to end the day with a sparkler and a smile.

¼ cup butter
1 onion, minced
1 tablespoon minced garlic
4 stalks celery, minced
¼ cup flour
1 (28-ounce) can San Marzano tomatoes
1 (28-ounce) can roasted red peppers
2 quarts lobster stock (see recipe, p. 208)
¼ cup dry sherry
1 lemon, cut in half
1 quart heavy cream
4 ounces smoked gouda, grated
1 tablespoon white pepper
¼ cup dill weed
1 tablespoon Old Bay seasoning
4 whole lobsters, cooked, meat removed, shells used in stock
¼ cup Pernod liqueur
Pernod cream for garnish (4 tablespoons heavy cream and 1 tablespoon Pernod)

lobster bisque

In a large soup pot, melt the butter, add the onion, garlic, and celery, and cook until just lightly caramelized. Sprinkle in the flour, stirring constantly. Cook for five minutes, then add the tomatoes and roasted red peppers. Slowly pour in your stock and wine while continuing to stir.

Add the lemon, then simmer for 1 hour to reduce ¼ of the stock. Take out the lemon, squeeze its juices into a cup, remove seeds, and pour the juice back into the pot.

With an immersion blender, puree the juice thoroughly, then pour it back into the pot and stir in the heavy cream, smoked gouda, spices, and pernod. Cook on low until flavors have blended.

When ready to serve, place the lobster meat in the center of a bowl or cup and ladle the hot soup over it. Garnish and drizzle with Pernod cream. Serve with a crusty french baguette.

For the bowl, garnish with shell; for the cup, serve with caviar toast.

Serves 10

lobster stock

1 1/2 gallon water
3 lemons, cut in half
1/3 cup Old Bay seasoning
12 bay leaves
4 whole lobsters

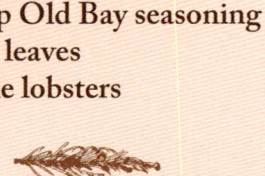

Bring the water, lemons, and spices to boil. Add the lobsters and boil for 10–15 minutes, depending on the size of the lobster (10 minutes for a 1-pound lobster, 15 minutes for a 1½- to 2-pound lobster. Take the lobster out of the pot, and let the water continue to simmer while you remove the meat from the shells.

Once the lobster has cooled to the touch, break it down, removing the meat to save for later. If you see any greenish "tomalley," or red "coral" eggs, you can choose to eat that spread on toast as a little treat or add it back to the stock for a richer flavor.

Add the shells back to the pot and continue to cook until reduced by a third. Strain through a colander.

Save the tail shells for garnish when serving the bisque in a bowl.

Makes approximately 2 quarts

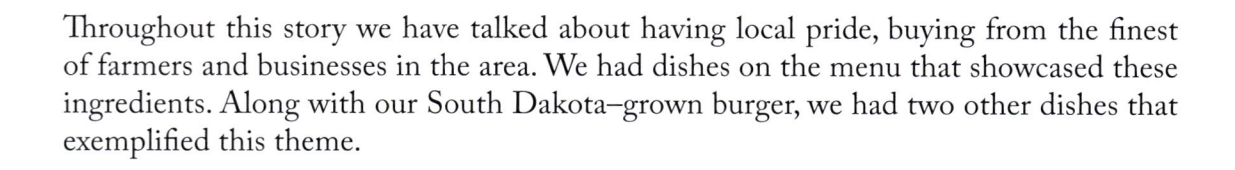

Throughout this story we have talked about having local pride, buying from the finest of farmers and businesses in the area. We had dishes on the menu that showcased these ingredients. Along with our South Dakota–grown burger, we had two other dishes that exemplified this theme.

dakota sausage beer mac

½ pound Hyatt Family Farm smoked local brat, sliced
½ red bell pepper, small diced
4 cups macNcheese (see recipe, p. 72)
4 ounces Fernson Lion's Paw Lager
¼ cup grated parmigiano reggiano
2 green onions, diced
¼ cup crushed pretzels

In a large sauté pan, lightly brown the sausage and red peppers. Fold in the macNcheese, and slowly add the beer. Cook only until warmed thoroughly, otherwise the noodles will get mushy. Put in a serving bowl and top with grated parmigiano, green onions, and pretzels.

Serves 2

dakota gumbo

½ pound butter
1 cup flour
2 yellow onions, diced
2 green peppers, diced
3 celery stalks, diced
4 pounds fresh tomatoes or 6 cups canned diced tomatoes
1 tablespoon cayenne pepper
3 tablespoon gumbo filé powder

3 large bay leaves
1 tablespoon minced garlic
7 cups pork broth
1 can Fernson farmhouse ale
1 pound okra, sliced
2 pound pheasant sausages, thick sliced
2 pound buffalo sausages, thick sliced
salt and pepper to taste
pickled okra for garnish

In a large pot, start making the roux: melt the butter, then slowly add the flour, stirring constantly on low heat until it's the color and consistency of peanut butter, approximately 20 minutes. The darker the roux, the richer the flavor.

Add your "holy trinity"—the onion, peppers, and celery—to the pot and stir well, then cook until the onions are translucent.

Then add the tomatoes and spices. Slowly stir as you add the broth and beer.

Bring to a boil, add the okra, then reduce heat and simmer on low until it thickens, about another hour.

In a sauté pan, brown sausage in 2 tablespoon olive oil, then add to the stockpot. Taste and season with salt and pepper as needed.

Serve with warm cooked rice. Garnish with pickled okra. We used vegetables from Mary's Kitchen and Gardens and sausages from Prairie Harvest.

Serves 10 - 12

Soup is good for the soul...

"Soup puts the heart at ease, calms down the violence of hunger, eliminates the tension of the day, and awakens and refines the appetite."

—*Auguste Escoffier*

This quote seems appropriate to describe the feeling that the women felt when they arrived at 6 p.m. every second Monday of the month. The gathering of the GrapeGals started off tense as they checked in, standing in line waiting for the first glass of wine. Once their table was filled with friends and the soup and cheese were out, a calm aura filled the room . . . until the cheerful effects of the wine kicked in.

The GrapeGals will always be dear to my heart. Not just because the group continued to meet for so many years, but because of the friendships and support for each other that formed. In the earlier years it was one wine rep that hosted the evening. I was proud to eventually bring them all together. Having the best women in the local wine industry as a team was invigorating. We learned so much from each other as we planned out what the theme would be. This synergy has continued beyond The Market doors.

"For women who celebrate the good things in life . . . wine, food, friends, and fun!" This was the GrapeGal motto, and ladies who came to these events upheld it with honor. Many of the women came every month, the perfect night out with their girlfriends. They were not only fans of the event but also loyal to The Market. It didn't have to be a GrapeGal night for them to come shopping or enjoying meals with friends and family. For this, and so much more, I will always be grateful.

Throughout the years we had winemakers visit, we painted pictures of wine glasses to grace the walls, had a bring-your-dog day, and hosted fundraisers for local charities. It was always something different. What didn't change was the ladies' love for the soup and cheese I would pair with the wine. When I asked for help listing their favorite soups, I was inundated with replies. Bev Austin was the champion, not only naming the soup but what cheese and wine were served with it, and the date we enjoyed it! While I couldn't possibly give you all the recipes, these were the most requested.

This first soup was addictive … easy to make, a great vegan option, it has a beautiful color and bright flavors that excite the palate!

curried carrot soup

2 yellow onions, diced
10 carrots, sliced
6 tablespoons grated ginger
2 tablespoons minced garlic
1 teaspoon red curry paste
2 tablespoons yellow curry powder
1 quart vegetable broth
1 (15-ounce) can coconut milk
salt and pepper
6 tablespoons toasted coconut
pea sprouts and green chili oil for garnish

In a stockpot, sauté the onions and carrots until soft. Add the ginger, garlic, curries, and vegetable broth. Simmer for 30 minutes. Using an immersion blender, puree the soup until creamy.

Stir in the coconut milk and toasted coconut. Season with salt and pepper to taste.

Garnish with a pea sprout, dot with green chili oil.

Serves 4

Most people have only experienced this next variety of soup in a can, usually only used in an old casserole recipe, certainly not something you would eat an entire bowl of, at least not until you try this recipe. I can't take credit for this delightful creation though; this is from Allen Wright, a surprisingly light yet full-flavored soup.

cream of celery soup

1 cup butter
1 cup flour
1½ quarts vegetable stock
3½ pounds chopped celery, save some leaves for garnish
1 yellow onion, chopped
6 carrots, finely chopped
4 cups milk
1 tablespoon minced garlic
1 tablespoon thyme
1 tablespoon rubbed sage
2 teaspoons celery salt
1 teaspoon white pepper
1 quart heavy cream
salt and pepper to taste

In a large stockpot, melt the butter. Gradually add the flour, always stirring. Allow the paste to bubble and begin to smell nutty. Continue to cook until lightly golden, around 5 minutes. Whisk in the vegetable stock, and allow to simmer on low as you prepare the vegetables.

Sauté the chopped vegetables until soft. Add to the thickening stock.

Stir in the milk and garlic. Bring to a boil, then lower heat and simmer for half an hour.

Take off heat. Using an immersion blender, puree the soup until creamy and no chunks of vegetable left. Add the spices and heavy cream. Return to heat, simmer for another 20 minutes. Season with salt and pepper to taste.

When serving, garnish the top with celery leaves.

Serves 4- 6

chicken mushroom soup

2 tablespoons olive oil
1 pound chicken breast, diced
2 yellow onions, diced
1 tablespoon thyme leaves
¾ tablespoons crushed pink peppercorns
1½ tablespoons sage leaves
2 tablespoons butter
4 ounces white rice
2 ounces wild rice
2 ounces couscous
1 ounce orzo
2 ounces dried split peas
½ tablespoon poppy seed
1 tablespoon minced garlic
1 teaspoon green hot sauce
6 stalks celery, diced
3 pounds assorted mushrooms, de-stemmed, broken in large pieces
10 cups chicken broth
salt and pepper to taste

In a sauté pan, heat the olive oil, add the chicken and onions, and season with thyme, pink peppercorns, and sage. Cook until browned.

Meanwhile, in a stockpot, melt the butter, add both of the rices, couscous, orzo, split peas, and poppy seed, and lightly roast to give it a nutty flavor. Add the garlic, hot sauce, celery, and mushrooms. Add the cooked chicken and onions.

Pour the chicken stock over the top and simmer until rice is cooked. Salt and pepper to taste.

portuguese pork and vegetable soup

2 pork shanks
½ pound lamb merguez sausage, cut in chunks
¾ pound chorizo links, cut in chunks
6 tomatoes, diced
2 yellow onions, diced
1 butternut squash, peeled and cut into bite-sized chunks
1½ quarts pork broth
1 (32-ounce) can tomato juice
1 (16-ounce) can chickpeas
1 pound kale, stemmed and chopped
2 tablespoons sherry vinegar
1 teaspoon liquid smoke
1 tablespoon sea salt
4 tablespoons cumin
1 tablespoon red pepper flakes
1 tablespoon cracked black pepper
6 tablespoons smoked paprika

In a stockpot, cover the pork shanks with water, put on the lid, and cook until the meat begins to fall off the bone. Remove, take the meat off the bone, and throw it back into the simmering juices.

Add the sausages, tomato, onion, and squash. Pour in the broth and tomato juice, cover, and simmer for 1 hour. Add the chickpeas, kale, sherry, liquid smoke, and spices, and simmer until flavors are rich.

Serves 8

Chapter Ten

dealing with a pandemic

facing the unknown...

Business at The Market was getting better with each passing year. Eventually we paid back our partners and were once again sole proprietors. Our plan was to invest all our time and effort to ensure the business would be our retirement fund. It appeared that our hard work was paying off.

We started 2020 at a record pace! The weather had been relatively mild, bringing out more diners than usual. Shauna, my wine rep from Republic National Distributing and I were planning a huge wine dinner with Grgich Hills Winery. John, from Okoboji Wines, brought in the rosé barrel samples so we could decide what we'd want to buy for the new vintage release. It looked like it was going to be another exciting year.

When word of Covid-19 first started breaking out, we were skeptically concerned, listening to the news to keep updated. Like many people, we thought this would be like a flu epidemic and pass within a few months. As precautions were announced, we cleared our tables of glasses and silverware. Flowers were replaced with sanitizer pumps. Gloves and masks became the new uniform. Brittany, one of our servers, was making colorful masks for us from vintage prints, trying to bring cheer to an uncomfortable circumstance.

As the situation escalated, we gathered the staff to share concerns. Many of them had health issues, young children at home, or were responsible for helping with the care of grandparents. The risks now were beginning to outweigh the need to work. At the same time, the city had already mandated only 50 percent occupancy and were closing down all indoor dining, only allowing takeout.

attempting take-out...

Our food was not conducive to being packed in a to-go container, but we had no choice if we were going to try to stay open. With a new plan of action, we sent the following post out on social media.

"During this time when our lives seem so unsure, we would like to send you home with a bit of comfort. We've put together a menu of take-out friendly dishes, including some of your favorites from our regular fare. Laurel will also begin offering special meals with instructions on how to prepare them in your own kitchen. Need the perfect wine, beer, or spirit pairings, we'll help you out with that also. Use us as personal shoppers, we'll help you with your selection, package it and deliver it out to your vehicle.

"If you wish to shop yourself, we have moved many of our food items from the gourmet room to the dining area to allow for safe social distancing. There will be daily specials posted on our Facebook page, so check us out often.

"We always appreciate your support, and hope that these changes will help ease a little stress and bring a little pleasure during these trying times."

We offered special pre-packed bags that had everything you needed for a "date night for two" at home. There was a choice of white or red wine. I selected a couple of cheeses, charcuterie, and something for a sweet treat that paired perfectly with the wine. The cotton candy cheesecake was a huge hit, bringing a smile to whomever received it.

cottoncandy frozen cheesecake

2 cups graham cracker crumbs
2 tablespoons sugar
1 stick butter
2 pounds cream cheese, softened
¼ cup shaved white chocolate, melted
½ cup sugar
1 cup heavy cream, whipped to stiff peaks
1 cup boiling water
2 tablespoons berry jello mix
2 tablespoons strawberry jello mix
1 cup white chocolate icing
1 small bag of cotton candy

Mix cracker crumbs, sugar, and melted butter.

Press crumb mixture into a springform pan, put in the freezer.

Blend cream cheese, white chocolate shavings and sugar until smooth, fold in whipped cream, divide it into 2 bowls, then put in the refrigerator.

Pour boiling water into 2 separate small cups, add berry jello in one, the strawberry jello in the other, stir well. Refrigerate until cool, but not congealed.

Add the berry jello into one of the cheesecake filling bowls, stir until well blended. Add additional jello powder to make the blue color desired.

Do the same steps with the strawberry jello.

Remove the spring-form pan from the freezer, alternately scoop the two fillings to form a marbling effect in the pan.

Place the pans back in the freezer to set overnight.

When ready to serve, cut into 12 pieces. Let it sit out for 15 minutes. Top with a drizzle of icing and puff of cotton candy.

Serves 12

As hard as we tried to adjust to the new Covid lifestyle, it was getting increasingly difficult to come in each day and keep a smile on our faces. The tense feeling when people came in was emotionally draining. Stand six feet apart, sanitize every pen after they sign the credit card slip, constantly wiping down the retail area, piles of used disposable gloves—this was no longer The Market experience.

I will never be able to thank Katie, my dining room manager, enough for her loyalty and perseverance during this time. Her make-the-best-of-it attitude was calming, not only for me but for all our customers. She ran through the dining room, across the patio. and down the stairs to deliver packages to people who didn't want to come in. Katie was truly an angel of mercy during such a tumultuous time.

In a state where the governor would not order a shut-down, it was left to the individual businesses to make that decision. Half of the general public had not yet taken the outbreak seriously; if you closed, you were thought of as a sheep and a quitter by this half of the population. The other half believed that if you stayed open you were a greedy, uncaring person. You were damned if you did and damned if you didn't. We decided to be sheep and try to do what was best for the flock.

This note was hung on the door and posted to our fans on Facebook: *"Thank you to everyone who ordered take out and supported us during this time, your kindness and generosity will never be forgotten. However, we've come to a heartfelt realization that to remain open could possibly contribute to the spread that our community is trying to stop. And so, as of today, we are closed until further notice. Our focus now is to spend this time planning exciting changes to our menu and future events. We hope to be back soon and enjoy a sunny patio season. Until then, stay safe, stay healthy & stay in touch!"* - ♥**The Market Family**♥

quarantine time...

Feeling that we'd done the right thing did not ease the sudden fear and loneliness that overwhelmed me for the first few weeks of being home. I was one of those that got attached to the television, having the news on all day long. Watching the daily infection and death counts was taking a toll on my faith that this was going to be a short sabbatical.

I must admit that Facebook was my therapy during this time. Not only did it keep me close to family, friends, and customers, but it offered ways to keep my passions alive and growing with virtual events. Not a master on the computer, I managed to figure out programs such as Zoom; sometimes my voice wasn't there, but I was still a part of something great.

I finally got myself back in the kitchen. First thing I cooked was my Gramma's chicken and noodles. I hadn't made it in years. As I was rolling out the dough and smelling the chicken and herbs simmering, I swear I felt her in the room. She was there to help ease the fears of losing my business and push me to start fighting for the reopening of it.

Words of Support

The downtown business organization designed a montage of fellow business owners holding up words of support to inspire us all that this would be over soon and collectively we'd all open our doors to new success.

The following month my efforts were focused on a new menu and how to reset The Market to accommodate any restrictions we might have upon reopening. After being closed for so long, cash flow would need to be fortified to be able to restock the now empty coolers. Liquor was one category of items that we really didn't have to carry, so I organized an online sale to clear that inventory. I was pleasantly surprised with the success of the virtual event.

We had a Zoom meeting with all the staff to see who would be ready to come back. It was a very emotional sight to see their faces again! I was looking forward to getting us all back together again, even if it was just for cleaning, for now.

and the doors reopen...

After two months, it was finally announced that restaurants could begin to start seating again. We were fortunate to have our large patio, knowing many people would feel more comfortable with outdoor dining. The retail was moved back into the shop area. Tables were put in place, keeping them at the six-foot spacing. Anything we could do to help ease the stress of re-entry was applied.

As much as I was looking forward to opening the doors again, there was an apprehension that lay at the surface. What if we opened too soon and there was a surge? Would they close us down again? Would people even want to come out to dine anymore now that they had gotten used to takeout? This was like opening a new business in so many ways.

But the day finally came, and ready or not, the key turned in the door and we were once again greeting guests. Many of us had not left the house for months, so it was an awkward first meeting, especially for the people we had known for so long. I am a big hugger, and had always greeted our regulars with arms open wide. Now as they came in, there was an uncomfortable pause, standing apart, welcoming with smiles hidden behind a mask.

I tried to push the discomfort to the back, escaping more often to the kitchen, where I felt some sort of normalcy. One of our beloved cooks, Jacob, made the decision to not return to the restaurant industry. He had been at our side, along with Katie, during the short takeout phase, and was greatly missed now. My extra help was appreciated by the other cooks because of this.

While back in the kitchen, I could also help them with the new dishes I had worked on during quarantine. We were so incredibly busy that opening week, it took us all by surprise. The kitchen crew had to get a flow again, plus learn new recipes. And the plate that was outselling them all was the curried halloumi bowl.

curried halloumi bowl

2 cups corn
2 tablespoons canned diced green chilis
24 slices fresh ginger root, thinly cut
4 cloves garlic, thinly sliced
2 tablespoons yellow curry powder
1 teaspoon red curry paste
3 tablespoons tahini
1 lime, juice and zest
1 (14-ounce) can coconut milk
1 (14-ounce) can garbanzo beans
2 (8-ounce) packages halloumi cheese
2 tablespoons olive oil
2 cups cooked white rice
1 english cucumber, thinly sliced
4 tablespoons fresh mint, chopped for garnish
2 green onions, sliced, or 4 tablespoons minced chives for garnish
sweety drop peppers for garnish

Combine the corn, chilis, ginger root, garlic, curries, tahini, lime, and coconut milk, and let sit.

Drain the garbanzo beans and dry with a paper towel. Cut the halloumi chunks in half. Warm the olive oil on medium heat in a large sauté pan. Cook the cheese on both sides until crispy brown. Remove, and cover to keep warm. Add the garbanzo beans to the same pan and cook until they start "popping."

Add the coconut milk mixture. Heat until completely warmed through.

Divide into 4 serving bowls. Top with a scoop of hot rice, a halloumi piece, and cucumber slices. Garnish with mint, green onions, and a couple of sweety drop peppers for color.

Serves 4

You normally make hummus with chickpeas, but we wanted to change things up a bit, so we switched to white beans. Surprisingly, it is a healthier option, with fewer calories and less fat than chickpeas. This plate was immensely popular on its own and when incorporated into other dishes.

white bean and artichoke hummus

½ cup extra virgin olive oil
8 cloves garlic
juice of 2 lemons
2½ pounds cooked navy beans (reserve 1 cup beans for garnish)
½ cup tahini
2 (14-ounce) cans artichoke heart quarters
¼ tablespoon cumin
½ tablespoon pink peppercorns
¼ cup bean water
¼ cup artichoke brine from can
½ tablespoon sea salt
2 preserved lemons, minced
¼ cup almond slivers
4 ounces feta crumbles
2 tablespoon za'atar
fresh chopped chives with blossoms and sweety drop peppers for garnish

Pre-prep: Place the olive oil and garlic cloves in a small sauté pan on low heat, cook until brown, and take off heat. Juice the lemons (if you roll the lemon on the counter, pressing down with your palm, you will feel the lemon soften, which will yield more juice).

Place the beans, tahini, 4 of the artichoke quarters, lemon juice, cumin, pink peppercorns, browned garlic cloves, and half the warmed oil from the pan into a food processor and mix until fully combined. Slowly add the remaining oil while the processor is running, and do the same with the bean water and artichoke brine until you get desired consistency. Add salt to your taste. The hummus will thicken more once chilled.

Presentation: When ready to serve, spoon the hummus in a circle, leaving an indent on one side to drizzle a pool of olive oil in. On the other side, place the remaining artichoke quarters, the preserved lemons, and the almonds. Top with reserved beans and the feta. Sprinkle with za'atar spice, then garnish with chives and peppers. Serve with grilled naan bread.

Serves 6 - 8

green goddess lamb chislic with hummus

1 pound lamb leg, cut into 1-inch cubes
chislic marinade (see recipe below)
1 cup hummus
avocado green goddess sauce
4 ounces feta crumbles for garnish
1 cucumber, sliced, for garnish
fresh rosemary and lemon wedges for garnish

Place the lamb in a bowl, cover with the marinade, and let sit for at least 3 hours.

Heat olive oil in a sauté pan, add the marinated lamb, and heat until medium-rare and browned on the outside.

Place the meat in the middle of two plates, spread hummus on one side, green goddess on the other.

Garnish with feta, cucumber, fresh rosemary, and lemon wedges. Serve with naan bread or pita, grilled.

Serves 2

chislic marinade

¼ cup olive oil
2 teaspoons worcestershire sauce
2 tablespoons minced fresh rosemary
¾ teaspoon kosher salt
1 tablespoon minced garlic
1 teaspoon cracked black pepper
2 tablespoons pinot noir

Combine all ingredients.

avocado green goddess sauce

1 avocados, mashed
3 ounces yogurt
1 ounce cilantro
1 ounce fresh basil
½ jalapeno, de-seeded & chopped
1 teaspoon dill weed
1 lemon, juice & zest

Mix all the ingredients in a food processor, pulsing lightly just to blend. Keep covered and cool.

It was wonderful to see the GrapeGals having fun again at the Mask-erade tasting. Some of our most loyal customers, The Hoppe's and Eric Schulte, were back on their stools at the end of the bar. I was happy to see my friends back on Saturday afternoons. Terry and Lynette along with Pete and Paula were shopping for the newest goodies. I always had something special that I'd share with them. Whether it was wine, groceries, or a new dish, I had a story to tell. Leighann was once again picking out pinot noirs for Brian and Amy. It almost made things feel like things were back to normal.

But they weren't. It was so hard to watch the girls run from the hot kitchen to the far end of the patio, trays full of food, struggling to catch a breath from under their masks. Doug was overworked in an understaffed kitchen. When the patio was full, people hesitated about sitting indoors. Large groups were not allowed, so the lower level remained empty. What would happen in September when we only had eight tables to seat guests?

I began to realize that the old way of life was not going to return, at least not for a very long time. It was beginning to feel like a job. Doug's frustration was also mounting. Before the pandemic, we had planned to sell or retire in two years. So, after a long, heartfelt conversation, we made the difficult decision to move that timeline up and retire now.

time to retire...

Once the decision was made, things moved so fast it was surreal. Telling the staff and our loyal regulars was heartrending. I felt like we were breaking up the band. But everyone was so understanding and supportive, it certainly helped me handle my separation anxiety.

Our last day of being open will always be special to me. The girls went to unlock the front door and yelled back to me that I better come out there. When I got close and saw all the people gathered on the patio, it took my breath away. Once I walked through the door, they started to applaud. It couldn't have been a better send-off. I had been working hard at not crying all week, but this broke the dam. It was a whirlwind of a day, breaking all the anti-hugging rules.

We would take a couple days off and start the process of selling everything. What a chore that would be; twenty years of accumulation is a lot to tag. I don't think you could title me a hoarder, but I do have a hard time throwing or giving things away. But with my chin up and my cheerful servers, Claire, Brittany, and Jamie by my side, we got through it.

We started the sale off with a day for friends and family to have the chance to shop before we opened it up to the general-public. The day turned into night; the sale turned into a party. We certainly made a dent in the remaining inventory.

The things that really meant a lot to me came home; the rest went to new places where they would be admired and taken care of. There were a couple of pieces of furniture that had deep sentimental value.

I had a butcher block table that had traveled from Mike's restaurants to all of mine. The wells and scratches had been forged from years of prepping. Running your hand over the top, you could only imagine all the knives that had left their mark. This is now in my kitchen at home, thanks to the very good friends who helped make that happen.

Then there were Don and Tammy. They would certainly win the Market attendance award. They had sat on the same stools at the end of the bar every time they came in, unless they were with a larger group. We even made name tags for their spot. So we called them down for one last glass of wine before we locked the doors for good. As we were leaving, I asked if they had forgotten something. They looked perplexed. I picked up their stools, explaining that they needed to go home with them. Another teary moment.

Two days later, the place was just about empty. Only the memories remained.

epilogue

With very few days remaining at The Harvester, I stood out on the patio reflecting on all the great meals that had been shared, all the wine that had been sipped on these grounds. There were numerous engagements and rehearsal dinners, along with three actual weddings. Birthdays, graduations, and anniversaries were all celebrated. Thinking about these special moments made me realize just how much I was going to miss being a part of making people's lives happy.

My deep thoughts were cut short by a friendly voice inquiring as to what The Market was. Explaining that the restaurant was closed, I gladly invited her in to hear my story. There just happened to be a chilled bottle of rosé at the ready, so after a quick tour, we settled in to chat at the bar.

Torund Bryhn had just entered my life. She had a way of making you open up, to feel pride in yourself and accomplishments. Before I knew it, I had agreed to go on her podcast, Moving Beyond Your Tribe. She talks with people of all walks of life, bringing out their inner thoughts on the path of their career and how it affects those around you. Getting you to step out of your comfort zone and create new opportunities is her superpower.

During our conversations she helped me to recognize that The Market was so much more than just another restaurant. It wasn't only about the food, it was about the relationships, the passion of sharing the good things in life. How would I satisfy this emotional undercurrent while retired?

I had already planned on writing a blog called "What's on My Palate", featuring my favorite new culinary finds along with reviews of local restaurants and shops. But, the stacks of recipes and folders filled with recipes called out to be preserved, to become a book. And as fate would have it, the lady that could help me accomplish this feat was sitting right next to me. Torund was the publisher at st. john's press. Thus began our partnership and my quest to create a feast of memories.

I turned the spare bedroom into my "inspiration room", surrounding myself with all the trinkets and books I've collected through the years. Thinking I would approach this as a job, going to the office so to speak, would keep me from procrastinating and form a routine that I sorely missed.

The day arrived where I would begin writing. With everything organized, I opened a new file, and all I could do was just stare at the empty screen…and cry. My old photo albums were stacked to my right of my computer, seemingly calling out to me. After a trip down memory lane, I knew why I had this writer's block. Creating this book was not a job, this would be an expression of gratitude to all that have been a part of this crazy, exciting journey I have been on.

Sitting at a desk was not going to allow my creativity to flow, so I moved all my recipes, photos, and boxes of memorability out to the living room. Here I built my ingenuity nest. I spent the winter snuggled into the couch with my favorite blanket, a bottle of wine at my side, and surrounded by piles of papers. My laptop became my best friend.

Before I knew it, this amazing book came together. Once I had to type in the recipes, I wanted to apologize to all my kitchen staff for the poorly written instructions. I realized that cooking comes so naturally to me that I just assumed everyone else would understand what I was describing. I had to remake many of the dishes to get accurate measurements. My home kitchen didn't even have measuring spoons or cups; guess what Doug got me for Christmas!

My "baby" was finally born, the pages had been written, now it was time to dress her up. Most cookbook covers consist of a picture of food or the chef. We wanted to be unique, to be one of the first to adorn a cover with a group of friends enjoying a feast. Torund sent the picture of a Renoir painting as inspiration, to recreate one of his most famous and complex paintings that immortalized his friends and special associates. The Luncheon of the Boating Party romanticizes friends enjoying food and wine together, exactly what I had attempted to accomplish at Food n' Fermentations and The Market.

Excited to once again be planning a party, I gathered my "luncheon ladies" to work out the details. I certainly missed having all the dishes and décor available, but with friends' help we all gathered the pieces to build our summer picnic atmosphere. With lights strung across the cabana, the tables covered in linens and flowers, it was finally time to greet the guests.

As each car pulled up to the picnic grounds the exhilaration rose. Seeing everyone walk up with a dish in one hand, a bottle in the other, and wearing a big smile, warmed my heart. A hug was their ticket to the event.

Gathered around the table were all good folks who had an instrumental part in my life and the success of The Market. It was humbling to hear the stories shared among them. This was the first time we all had been together since Doug and I retired. It was like going back in time and we were at one of our wine dinners. The sound of wine glasses tinging with each toast, the smell of salmon on the grill, and the sight of this nostalgic feast was extraordinarily pleasing.

We put out a journal to allow our guests to pen their thoughts. The emotional read summed up what we all felt, there is never going to be another market. We go from restaurant to restaurant in hopes of finding a new place that will evoke that camaraderie, that will challenge your palate as we did.

I hope we find it someday, but in the meanwhile, the memories will never fade. The passion for wine and food that I hope I helped to instill in all of you will continue to grow. I no longer have the brick and mortar to channel my talents but that will not stop me from sharing the best wine, food and spirits with you and others.

This book is not a closure, it is only the beginning of a new way of sharing my culinary experiences and recipes. I have at least two books inside of me and years of new adventures ahead.

laurel lather's bio

Laurel Lather was a popular chef and culinary entrepreneur for close to three decades in downtown Sioux Falls. Her first gourmet food and wine shoppe, Food n' Fermentations, laid the groundwork for the success of The Market, her favorite project located in the historic Harvester building. This was a two-story restaurant with an expansive garden patio, a wine and cheese shop, and an event room.

During this time, Laurel enjoyed being a contributing writer for local publications such as Now!Pavilion and Wholesome Magazines. She also wrote light-hearted wine reviews for The Argus Leader's wine blog section.

Prior to this, Laurel lived in her home state of Wisconsin. She opened her first business at the age of 22, Laurel's Country Herbs, then a year later, opening The General Store, a bulk grocery & local produce shop. This passion eventually leads her to the restaurant industry, working in some of Chippewa Falls most popular restaurants until moving to South Dakota.

Being a consummate lover of food culture, retirement has not stopped Laurel from being a part of the local epicurean scene. The friendships she nurtured with her sales reps keeps her in the-know. She visits area restaurants and small ethnic groceries, writing reviews and posting dishes prepared with items purchased. You can read about her explorations at "What's on my Palate".

This is Laurel's first book, with plans for a "feast series."

praise

"Laurel Lather's Nostalgic Feast is a pure joy to read. Much more than a cookbook, this tours de force chronicles Laurel's evolution as a chef still embracing her Midwestern routes but also exploring and mastering cuisine from around the world. This book is a must have for every person that enjoys good food in the company of friends and family."

-Eric Schulte

"Nostalgic Feast stays true to its first sentence as a beautifully written tale of how food isn't just a small part of every day, it's a big part of our life. As a culinary legend in Sioux Falls, Laurel's restaurants were a part of so many people's stories and now the book can become part of their stories too! As a beginner cook myself, I love the ease and simplicity of this book, it makes me believe that I can create delicious food right from my home, while making my own memories."

-Sadie Swier

Community Outreach Coordinator

Downtown Sioux Falls, Inc.

"I have been frequenting Laurel's impressive stores and restaurants for over 25 years. She has been instrumental in reviving the food scene in Sioux Falls. Laurel always seeks out the very best ingredients and has a rare talent for creating a beautiful experience from conception to finish. I love her food and Nostalgic Feast is a fantastic expression of her passion as an extraordinary chef."

-Stacy Newcomb

Owner

Parker's Bistro

"Nostalgic Feast is so much more than a cookbook. It is a story about Laurel and her love of cooking amazing food and sharing those recipes with her family and friends."

–Lynette and Terry Kelley

"This book is such a treasure! I loved learning about Laurel's history and how she evolved into the talented chef that she is today. It reminds me of all the memories that were made her in her restaurants. We celebrated birthdays, anniversaries, and enjoyed Friday nights with friends sharing our favorite dishes. Nostalgic Feast will become my go-to cookbook now that I have the recipes to recreate the tastes I so enjoyed in my own home."

–Roseann Burchette

"As a fresh-out-of-college fast food addict, Laurel Lather exposed me to culinary creations the likes of which I had only dreamed about. She challenged me to try exotic wines and new-to-me foods. The recipes Laurel presents in Nostalgic Feast, will captivate, and tantalize your taste buds."

–Dena Espenscheid

Director of Grassroots Coalitions

Leadership Institute

"I am grateful to share in the nostalgia of one of my all-time favorite chefs. I first enjoyed Laurels cooking as a child and continued to pursue her restaurants as an adult where I have been blessed enough to bring my own children. What a treat to bring her detailed yet bountiful dishes to my own home. We look forward to cooking our way through this book."

–Jessica Kerher

Co-Owner/ Founder

Serendipitous Events

"I love how Nostalgic Harvest is written. Laurel paints a vivid picture with her stories of the past, it makes me feel like I am with her family as they are cooking. It's the same comfortable feeling of family Amy and I had when we would walk into her restaurant, The Market. We will cherish this book because Laurel is a creative chef, and we miss her food. More importantly, we will cherish this book because it will keep us connected to a person we love and miss!"

–Brian & Amy Clausen

"I've had the pleasure of dining at Laurel's restaurant numerous times, especially for wine dinners where her creativity was at its peak. I was thrilled to learn more about one of my favorite chefs through this memoir and attempt to recreate some of her treasurers in my own home. This will be a top of the counter cookbook for me!"

–Becky Blue

owner/vintner

Handwritten and Jessup Cellars Wines

"We've been fans of Laurel's cooking from the beginning. All our favorite dates and big life moments (like picking our children's names) were around her tables. Our love language is good food, gathered around the table with people we adore. Nostalgic Feast embodies those feelings and memories. I can't wait to host my own dinner party and recreate these recipes for my family and friends!"

–Marie & Bart Plocher

"Nostalgic Feast adds new depth to the many dining experiences we have enjoyed with Laurel. They have become even more special now that they are surrounded by her memories!"

–Pete and Paula Vogelsang

recipe index

A

Aioli:
- baconaisse, 168
- black garlic aioli, 150
- caper aioli, 79
- chipotle aioli, 165

Apple:
- apple strudel, 96
- salted caramel apple pie, 131

Appetizers:
- beer-battered cheese curds, 41
- beet deviled eggs, 76
- blistered black garlic shishito pepper, 151
- caprese oysters, 64
- confit of pheasant rillettes, 108
- deviled eggs, 75
- flower fritters, 29
- fried onion & bacon deviled eggs, 76
- honey cajun grilled oysters, 63
- italian meatball skillet, 177
- kimchi deviled eggs, 75
- oysters with mignonette, 65
- oysters rockefeller, 62
- rabbit and white truffle confit on toast, 158
- spring pea deviled eggs, 76
- t-rex wings, 48
- white bean and artichoke hummus, 225

Artichoke:
- grilled lemon chicken, 81
- white bean and artichoke hummus, 225

Avocado:
- avocado green goddess sauce, 227
- guacamole, 174
- guacAmole burger, 173

B

Bacon:
- baconaisse, 168
- bacon jam, 193
- bacon tomato jam, 166
- bourbon caramel bacon sundae, 134
- fried onion & bacon deviled eggs, 76
- peachy spinach and bacon salad with blue cheese dressing, 82
- sam's ultimate bacon grilled cheese sandwich, 182

Bass:
- white truffle bluenose bass with cassoulet, 156

Beans:
- cassoulet, 157
- chris's chickpea of the sea, 195
- curried halloumi bowl, 224
- green goddess lamb chislic with hummus, 226
- white bean and artichoke hummus, 225

Beets:
- beet and black garlic soup with beetgreen pesto and ginger crème, 148
- beet caprese with juniper pork belly, 185
- beet deviled eggs, 76
- beetgreen pesto, 149

Beef:
    black garlic prime rib sandwich, 150
Blackberry:
    spring duck and blackberry salad, 115
Black Garlic:
    beet and black garlic soup with beetgreen pesto and ginger crème, 148
    black garlic aioli, 150
    black garlic prime rib sandwich, 150
    blistered black garlic shishito pepper, 151
Blueberry:
    blueberry brie pie, 129
Blue Cheese:
    doug's blue cheese dressing, 83
Buffalo:
    sd grown burger, 167
Burgers:
    beer lover's burger, 171
    blt burger, 166
    elke sommer burger, 171
    guacAmole burger, 173
    holiday burger, 168
    honeybee burger, 176
    market charcuterie burger, 163
    napa cabernet burger, 160
    pepper lover's burger, 165
    sd grown burger, 167
    zinfandelic swiss and mushroom burger, 170

C

Cabbage:
    sauerkraut, 13
Caramel:
    bourbon caramel bacon sundae, 134
    bourbon caramel sauce, 135
    pork belly with pork caramel and spring veggies, 184
    pork caramel sauce, 184
    salted caramel apple pie, 131
Carrot:
    curried carrot soup, 212
Celery:
    cream of celery soup, 213
Cheese:
    beer-battered cheese curds, 41
    beer cheese sauce, 172
    beet caprese with juniper pork belly, 185
    blueberry brie pie, 129
    caprese grilled cheese, 138
    cheddar mashers, 113
    curried halloumi bowl, 224
    dakota sausage beer mac, 209
    doug's blue cheese dressing, 83
    grilled PBJBrie, 129
    macNcheese, 72
    marigold cheese soup, 31
    mushroom brie soup, 128
    sam's ultimate bacon grilled cheese sandwich, 182
    strawberry brie french toast with pink peppercorn cream, 127
    summer caprese salad, 139
    truffled macNcheese, 154
    truffle grilled cheese, 152
    whiskey braised onion and cheese soup, 111
    winter potted caprese, 136
    zinfandelic swiss and mushroom burger, 170
Chicken:
    chicken mushroom soup, 214
    gramma helen's chicken and homemade noodles, 20

    grilled lemon chicken, 81
Chili:
    spicy garden pepper chili, 51
Chocolate:
    eggplant chocolate torte, 147
Condiments:
    baconaisse, 168
    black garlic aioli, 150
    caper aioli, 79
    chipotle aioli, 165
    cranberry ketsup, 169
    pickled mustard seed, 163
    spicy honey butter, 176
Corned Beef:
    cold brew irish whiskey glazed corned beef, 112
    whole yellow pea soup, 23
Cranberry:
    cranberry ketsup, 169
    cranberry sauce, 91
    turkey cranberry sandwich, 90

D

Desserts:
    bourbon caramel bacon sundae, 134
    cottoncandy frozen cheesecake, 220
    eggplant chocolate torte, 147
    fruit stuffed baked tomato with ice cream, 140
    strawberry brie french toast with pink peppercorn cream, 127
Deviled Eggs:
    beet deviled eggs, 76
    deviled eggs, 75
    fried onion & bacon deviled eggs, 76
    kimchi deviled eggs, 75
    spring pea deviled eggs, 76

Duck:
    spring duck and blackberry salad, 115

E

Edible Flowers:
    flower fritters, 29
    marigold cheese soup, 31
    summer floral herb salad, 30
    wilted dandelion salad, 32
Eggs:
    beet deviled eggs, 76
    deviled eggs, 75
    fried onion & bacon deviled eggs, 76
    kimchi deviled eggs, 75
    spring pea deviled eggs, 76
Eggplant:
    calabrese flatbread, 74
    eggplant chocolate torte, 147
    eggplant parmigiano, 145
Elk:
    elke sommer burger, 171
    pulled elk roast, 106

F

Fish:
    halibut in harissa broth, 205
    halibut summer solstice salad, 188
    herbed halibut and veggie packet, 204
    lemon peppered walleye sammie, 78
    poached orange roughy with sauteed vegetables, 39
    white truffle bluenose bass with cassoulet, 156

G

Goat:
   moroccan goat curry with hummato, 117

H

Halibut:
   halibut in harissa broth, 205
   halibut summer solstice salad, 188

J

Jams & Jellies:
   bacon jam, 193
   bacon tomato jam, 166
   fresh strawberry jam, 18

L

Lamb:
   chislic marinade, 226
   green goddess lamb chislic with hummus, 226
   guacAmole burger, 173

Lemon:
   grilled lemon chicken, 81

Lobster:
   lobster bisque, 207
   lobster stock, 208

M

Martini:
   caprese martini, 137

Meatballs:
   italian meatballs, 178
   italian meatball skillet, 177
   swedish meatballs, 179
   swedish meatballs in gravy, 178

Mushrooms:
   chicken mushroom soup, 214
   mushroom brie soup, 128
   pheasant with morel mushrooms, 107
   vegan "pulled pork" sandwich, 196
   zinfandelic swiss and mushroom burger, 170

N

Nuts:
   candied walnuts, 135
   sweet potato pecan pie, 132
   vegan mac & cheese, 196

O

Onions:
   beer-braised onions, 172
   coffee braised onions, 167
   fried onion & bacon deviled eggs, 76
   pickled red onions, 79
   whiskey braised onion and cheese soup, 111

Oranges:
   yuzu orange salmon salad, 186

Orange Roughy:
   poached orange roughy with sauteed vegetables, 39

Oysters:
   caprese oysters, 64
   honey cajun grilled oysters, 63
   oyster and sea asparagus chowder, 65
   oysters with mignonette, 65
   oysters rockefeller, 62

P

Parsnip:
   green tomato parsnip soup with scallops, 141

Pasta Dishes:
   dakota sausage beer mac, 209
   elaine's lasagna, 104
   gramma helen's chicken and homemade noodles, 20
   macNcheese, 72
   truffled macNcheese, 154

Peaches:
   peachy spinach and bacon salad with blue cheese dressing, 82

Peas:
   spring pea deviled eggs, 76
   whole yellow pea soup, 23

Peppers:
   blistered black garlic shishito pepper, 151
   elaine's green chili sauce, 105
   pepper lover's burger, 165

Pheasant:
   confit of pheasant rillettes, 108
   pheasant with morel mushrooms, 107

Pickled Vegetables:
   bread and butter pickles, 14
   pickled mustard seed, 163
   pickled red onions, 79
   red wine pickles, 15

Pies:
   blueberry brie pie, 129
   finally worked pie crust, 132
   green tomato pie, 142
   rhubarb tarragon pie, 133
   salted caramel apple pie, 131
   sweet potato pecan pie, 132

Pork:
   beet caprese with juniper pork belly, 185
   elaine's green chili sauce, 105
   italian pulled pork, 193
   pork belly with pork caramel and spring veggies, 184
   pork caramel sauce, 184
   portuguese pork and vegetable soup, 215
   pos's pulled pork, 191
   three pigs and a duck, 192
   whipped lardo, 192

Potatoes:
   bangers and colcannon with irish whiskey glaze, 110
   cheddar mashers, 113
   truffle parmigiano chips, 154

R

Rabbit:
   rabbit and white truffle confit on toast, 158

Rhubarb:
   rhubarb scones, 18
   rhubarb tarragon pie, 133
   salad juliana: roasted rhubarb and herb salad, 189

S

Salad Dressings:
   doug's blue cheese dressing, 83
   ginger herb vinaigrette, 190
   spring duck and blackberry salad, 115
   watermelon vinaigrette, 31
   yuzu-kosho dressing, 187

Salads:
   halibut summer solstice salad, 188

peachy spinach and bacon salad with blue cheese dressing, 82
salad juliana: roasted rhubarb and herb salad, 189
summer caprese salad, 139
summer floral herb salad, 30
wilted dandelion salad, 32
winter potted caprese, 136
yuzu orange salmon salad, 186

Salmon:
herbed halibut and veggie packet, 204
hop-smoked salmon, 199
yuzu orange salmon salad, 186

Sandwiches:
black garlic prime rib sandwich, 150
calabrese flatbread, 74
caprese grilled cheese, 138
chris's chickpea of the sea, 195
grilled PBJBrie, 129
italian focaccia torte, 91
italian pulled pork, 193
lemon peppered walleye sammie, 78
sam's ultimate bacon grilled cheese sandwich, 182
three pigs and a duck, 192
truffle grilled cheese, 152
turkey cranberry sandwich, 90
vegan "pulled pork" sandwich, 196

Sauces:
avocado green goddess sauce, 227
beer cheese sauce, 172
beetgreen pesto, 149
black truffle tapenade, 153
cranberry sauce, 91
elaine's green chili sauce, 105
elaine's quick spaghetti sauce, 104
mole sauce, 173
our basil pesto, 143

pork caramel sauce, 184
red wine redux sauce, 160
t-rex sauce, 49
zinfandel demi-glaze, 170
Sauerkraut, 13

Sausage:
bangers and colcannon with irish whiskey glaze, 110
dakota gumbo, 209
dakota sausage beer mac, 209
hunter's stew, 93
portuguese pork and vegetable soup, 215

Scallops:
green tomato parsnip soup with scallops, 141

Scones:
rhubarb scones, 18

Sea Asparagus:
oyster and sea asparagus chowder, 65

Seafood:
green tomato parsnip soup with scallops, 141
lobster bisque, 207
lobster stock, 208
seafood boil for two, 202

Seasonings:
basil crystals, 144
herb de provence, 27
italian seasoning, 27
sage stuffing spice, 169
salt substitute, 27
zaatar for vegetables, 27

Soups:
beet and black garlic soup with beetgreen pesto and ginger crème, 148
chianti tomato basil soup, 71
chicken mushroom soup, 214
cream of celery soup, 213

    curried carrot soup, 212
    green tomato parsnip soup with scallops, 141
    lobster bisque, 207
    lobster stock, 208
    marigold cheese soup, 31
    mushroom brie soup, 128
    oyster and sea asparagus chowder, 65
    portuguese pork and vegetable soup, 215
    whiskey braised onion and cheese soup, 111
    whole yellow pea soup, 23

Spinach:
    oysters rockefeller, 62
    peachy spinach and bacon salad with blue cheese dressing, 82

Stews:
    dakota gumbo, 209
    hunter's stew, 93

Strawberry:
    fresh strawberry jam, 18
    strawberry brie french toast with pink peppercorn cream, 127

Strudel:
    apple strudel, 96

Sweet Potatoes:
    sweet potato pecan pie, 132

T

Tomatoes:
    bacon tomato jam, 166
    caprese grilled cheese, 138
    caprese oysters, 64
    chianti tomato basil soup, 71
    fruit stuffed baked tomato with ice cream, 140
    green tomato parsnip soup with scallops, 141
    green tomato pie, 142
    summer caprese salad, 139
    winter potted caprese, 136

Truffle:
    black truffle tapenade, 153
    rabbit and white truffle confit on toast, 158
    truffled macNcheese, 154
    truffle grilled cheese, 152
    truffle parmigiano chips, 154
    white truffle bluenose bass with cassoulet, 156

Turkey:
    t-rex wings, 48
    turkey cranberry sandwich, 90

V

Vegan Dishes:
    chris's chickpea of the sea, 195
    curried carrot soup, 212
    vegan mac & cheese, 196
    vegan "pulled pork" sandwich, 196

W

Walleye:
    lemon peppered walleye sammie, 78

Watermelon:
    watermelon vinaigrette, 31